Biblical Blocks

Inspired Designs for Quilters

ROSEMARY MAKHAN

Martingale
& COMPANY

Dedication

This book is lovingly dedicated to the memory of my mother, Ruth, and to her sisters, Marion, Jessie, Edith, and Greta Wallace. These are the women whose exemplary lives influenced and fostered me in my youth.

Acknowledgments

Special thanks to Josie Abel, Patricia Dear, Ruth Landon, Myrna Schott, and Carole Jean Stockhausen for sharing their quilts in this book. Thanks also to Ermy Akers and Jean Welbourn for their help with the Tree of Life quilt.

A big thank you to my family, Chris, Candice, and Kenneth for their helpfulness and encouragement.

Thanks also to the staff at Martingale & Company for their patience and faith in me.

That Patchwork Place® is an imprint of Martingale and Company™.

Martingale & Company
20205 144th Ave. NE
Woodinville, WA 98072-8478

Biblical Blocks: Inspired Designs for Quilters
©1993, 2001 by Rosemary Makhan
First edition 1993.
Second edition 2001.

Printed in Hong Kong
06 05 04 03 02 01   6 5 4 3 2 1

Mission Statement

We are dedicated to providing quality products and service by working together to inspire creativity an to enrich the lives we touch.

Credits

President…Nancy J. Martin
CEO…Daniel J. Martin
Publisher…Jane Hamada
Editorial Director…Mary V. Green
Editorial Project Manager…Tina Cook
Design and Production Manager…Stan Green
Technical Editors…Susan I. Jones and Jane Townswick
Copy Editor…Liz McGehee
Illustrator…Laurel Strand
Photographer…Brent Kane
Cover and Text Designer…Regina Girard

Library of Congress Cataloging-in-Publication Data Available

ISBN 1-56477-390-6

CONTENTS

INTRODUCTION

I have been interested in biblical themes as far back as I can remember. One of my earliest memories is of my mother reading Bible stories to my younger brother and me at bedtime. The one that made the most vivid impression on my young mind was the stoning of Stephen. I clearly remember crying myself to sleep afterward because I associated the story with my oldest brother, Stephen, and I imagined how our family would feel if such a terrible thing happened to him.

As I read and studied Bible stories in church and Sunday school and while attending university, I developed a real love for biblical themes. I was rather surprised when I started making quilts and realized that quite a number of quilt patterns had biblical names. One day, I decided to look through my quilting books and make a list of all the blocks that had a biblical connotation. I was amazed that there were enough and more to make a biblical sampler quilt.

One of my favorite patterns is the Tree of Life. Since this block was much larger than the rest, I decided that my quilt should be a medallion quilt with the Tree of Life at its center. Jesus said, "I am the Way, the Truth, and the Life" (John 14:6) and since this is the central, unifying theme of all Christian denominations, the idea seemed particularly appropriate.

The 20" Tree of Life medallion is surrounded by sixteen 9" blocks, each based on a biblical theme. An appliquéd border in the graceful Rose of Sharon pattern completes the quilt.

The different "striped" designs used in the blocks and borders of the quilt on the front cover of this book were all cut from one fabric with different designs printed vertically in stripelike fashion. Photos of quilts featuring other "striped" fabrics are included in the book for your inspiration. Before selecting the striped fabric for your quilt and cutting the pieces, be sure to read the directions for working with stripes on pages 12–13.

Not all of the twenty-one blocks shown in this book were used in the cover quilt. Extra blocks are labeled "alternate" blocks. These appear in the other quilts featured. Choose your favorite blocks to create your version of this biblical sampler quilt.

I hope you will enjoy making and sharing a biblical sampler quilt with your family and friends. I have included a Bible verse that I feel is appropriate for each block. You may wish to do further reading as you make each block. I found this additional knowledge enhanced my enjoyment of this project.

In the Beginning
Finished size: 90" x 90"

Made by Patricia Dear, 1995, Mississauga, Ontario, Canada

This quilt was awarded First Prize at the Mississauga Quilters' Guild show in September of 1995. It has very special meaning to Patricia, as it was used to drape the coffin of her sister who passed away several years ago from breast cancer. It was also used in a similar manner at her father's funeral. Patricia explains, "It seemed appropriate that the quilt with such a special religious meaning be used in this manner. The Tree of Life in its central position gave comfort." Patricia says she was overwhelmed by the number of people who commented on the beauty of her quilt and its special meaning to her.

Biblical Blocks Baby Quilt

Finished size: 51" x 61"

Made by Carole Jean Stockhausen, 1996, Northville, Michigan, U.S.
Made with help from Carole's quilt group, Hands All Around.

Carole made this delightful red-and-green quilt for her friend, Sharon Williams, and Sharon's fourth child, Kevin. Since Carole and Sharon had been in Bible Study class together for many years, the biblical theme was just perfect. The Rose of Sharon border made it even more special. This quilt would make a lovely Christmas wall hanging.

Biblical Blocks

Finished size: 88" x 88"

Made by Myrna Schott, 1997, Elmira, Ontario, Canada

The colors Myrna chose for her quilt are symbolic: green for the vegetation on
the earth, blues for the life-giving waters, royal purples and silver overprinted
fabric to signify the majesty and kingship of the Creator.

Biblical Album

Finished size: 80" x 80"

Made by Ruth Landon, 1993, Oakville, Ontario, Canada

Ruth says making this quilt brought back sentimental memories of Bible stories and Sunday school when she was small. She likes having the quilt hung in her living room, where she often sits and admires the intricate blocks.

Biblical Blocks

Finished size: 90" x 90"

Made by Josie Abel, 1993, Mississauga, Ontario, Canada

Josie says enthusiasm and perserverence paid off as her quilt won
Best of Show at the Mississauga Quilters' Guild show in 1995.

Biblical Blocks

Finished size: 90" x 90"

Made by Rosemary Makhan, 1993, Burlington, Ontario, Canada

This quilt was made in memory of Rosemary's mother, Ruth, who passed away on June 23, 1986—the day before Rosemary's birthday. Remembering her mother's strength gives Rosemary strength today. In 1993, "Biblical Blocks" was the Viewers Choice winner at the Country Quilt Fest, which was held at the Ontario Agricultural Museum in Milton, Ontario.

Tree of Life Wall Quilt

Finished size: 57½" x 57½"

Made by Rosemary Makhan, 2000, Burlington, Ontario, Canada.
Machine quilted by Ermy Akers of The Quilter's Cupboard in Burlington.

Jean Welbourn graciously allowed Rosemary to use her completed
Tree of Life block as a starting point for this quilt.

GENERAL DIRECTIONS

The general directions included here contain all the information necessary to plan and complete this special quilt.

Step-by-step cutting and sewing directions are given for each block and the border. Follow the directions carefully. Be sure to cut the pieces for the borders (page 17) before you cut the pieces for each block.

Fabric Selection

Consult the color photos of the quilts for help in selecting your fabrics. For best results, use 100% cotton fabrics that have been washed to remove sizing and to ensure that the colors will not run. Six fabrics were used to make the cover quilt: ecru for the background; dark blue, medium blue, navy blue, and green for the blocks and central medallion; and a "striped" fabric for borders and accents in the blocks. These colors were used in the directions for the quilt, but feel free to substitute your own favorites. Yardage requirements are based on a usable width of 42" after preshrinking. You will probably have some fabric left over to add to your collection.

The "striped" fabric is actually printed with several coordinating designs in a stripelike fashion. Throughout the directions in this book, it is referred to as "the striped fabric." Where portions of the striped fabric are used in the blocks, it may not look like a stripe at all. As you can see, careful planning and selective cutting of the borders and pieces in the blocks results in wonderful effects.

You may substitute a print or a solid for the striped fabric if you wish, but if you want to duplicate the quilts shown, select the striped fabric first. Look for a fabric printed with vertical stripes of various widths and designs. Then, select your background fabric and three or four additional prints for the blocks.

The striped fabric used had three different striped designs, each repeated at least four times across the width of the fabric for a total of twelve stripes or more. For the outer border, use the widest striped design plus the two narrow ones on each side of it. The same striped design surrounds the completed Tree of Life medallion. For the border just inside the appliquéd border and the one that surrounds the Tree of Life in the medallion, use a slightly narrower striped design.

Cutting

Rotary cutting is recommended for most of the pieces in this quilt, but you will need to make templates for cutting the block pieces from the striped fabric and for some shapes that have irregular measurements. All cutting measurements include ¼"-wide seam allowances. (For a refresher course on rotary cutting, see *Shortcuts: A Concise Guide to Rotary Cutting* by Donna Lynn Thomas.)

Making Templates for Pieced Blocks

Template patterns for the patchwork blocks are included when necessary. All of these template patterns include ¼"-wide seam allowances.

1. Trace the template patterns onto clear or frosted plastic to make durable, accurate templates. You can mark on plastic template material with a fine-line permanent marking pen, which makes an accurate line that will not smudge.

2. Mark the template number and grain-line arrow on each template. This line is necessary for correctly aligning the template with the grain line or the striped design on your fabric.

Cutting Striped Pieces

When cutting border strips from the striped fabric, be sure ¼"-wide seam allowances fall on either side of the desired stripe.

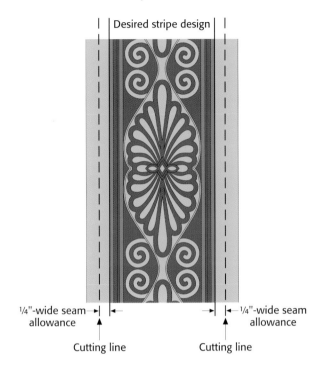

To cut identical pieces from striped fabric, make a template from transparent plastic and position it on the design area that you wish to include.

If desired, mark key fabric design areas directly onto the template. You can then easily position the template so each piece is identical.

Some blocks require the reverse of a template, indicated by the word "reversed" in the cutting directions. To reverse a template, simply turn it over before tracing around it.

Appliqué

The patterns for the Rose of Sharon border appliqués on page 72 do not include seam allowances. Use freezer paper to make precise appliqué pieces. The paper sticks to the fabric and controls the shape, helping to create perfectly shaped appliqués.

1. Place the freezer paper, coated side down, on the pattern. Trace each appliqué design with a sharp pencil.

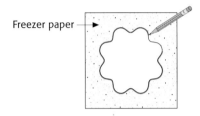

2. Cut out the freezer-paper shape on the pencil line. Do not add seam allowances.

3. Place the waxy side of the freezer paper against the wrong side of the appliqué fabric. Iron the freezer-paper shape to the wrong side of the fabric, using a dry iron set on "cotton."

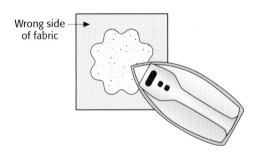

4. Cut out the fabric shape, adding a ³⁄₁₆"- or scant ¼"-wide seam allowance as you cut.

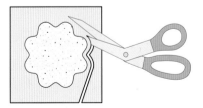

5. Fold the seam allowance snugly over the freezer paper to form the appliqué shape. Hand baste the seam allowance down, stitching through the paper, or glue the seam allowance to the freezer paper, using a fabric glue stick.

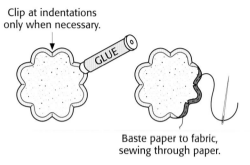

Clip at indentations only when necessary.

Baste paper to fabric, sewing through paper.

6. Pin or glue the shape to the background fabric, using the pattern as a placement guide.

7. Appliqué the shapes onto the background fabric. Use sewing threads which exactly match the appliqué fabrics. Take small invisible stitches that just catch the fold along the edge of the appliqué pieces.

8. Remove any basting stitches. Carefully make a slit behind each appliqué shape. Remove the freezer paper. (If you have used glue, it may be necessary to soak the piece in lukewarm water for five minutes to dissolve the glue first.)

9. Press the completed appliqué from the wrong side first, then "touch up" from the right side.

10. Carefully cut away the background fabric behind the appliqué, leaving a ¼"-wide allowance inside the piece.

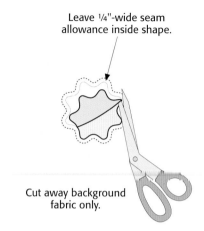

Leave ¼"-wide seam allowance inside shape.

Cut away background fabric only.

Preparing Bias Stems

Wonderfully fine bias stems are amazingly simple to make. Start by cutting several ½"-wide bias strips from your green fabrics. As you are cutting each bias strip, the edge of the fabric should just be barely visible along the outside edge of the ½" ruler markings. To estimate how many bias strips you will need for your project, lay some lengths of cut bias strips down roughly over the drawn stems on the pattern you have selected.

Lightly spray the bias strips with spray sizing, a product that is similar to spray starch but not as heavy. Spray the bias strips until they are slightly damp, but not wet. I like to put about four bias strips at a time into a small plastic bag and spray them at the same time, gently moving the strips around until they are evenly coated with spray sizing.

Using a Clover ¼" (6 mm) bias tape maker (the only brand that works well for this technique), insert the diagonal tip of one bias strip into the wide end of the tape maker. The right side of the fabric should be facing up, so that you can see it through the slot on top of the tape maker. Use a long straight pin to coax the bias fabric strip through the tape maker until it starts to come out the small end. Keep the bias strip centered as it goes into the wide end of the bias tape maker and make sure that the cut edges of the folded bias strip meet at the center when the strip is pressed. Turn the tape maker over and slowly pull on the handle while pressing the folded bias strip with a hot steam iron set on cotton. Be careful not to stretch the bias strip, and use the side of the iron, keeping it as close as possible to the tape maker.

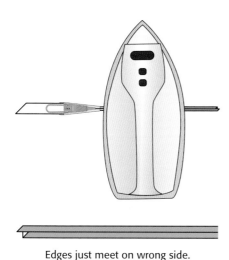

Edges just meet on wrong side.

Set-in Seams

Several of the blocks in this quilt require set-in seams. Set-in seams are seams with inside corners or angles. When the only way to add a piece to a block is to stitch it in two stages, you must use a set-in seam. All of the star blocks have set-in squares and triangles.

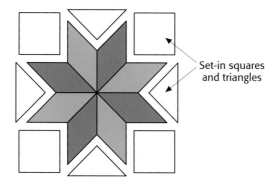

Set-in squares and triangles

This type of seam is usually sewn from the inside corner to the outer edge and is also known as Y-seam construction. Directions for adding pieces that require set-in seams are included with each block as needed.

To prepare pieces for set-in seams, mark the ¼" seam intersections at the outer corners and the inside corner of the pieces to be joined. Mark a tiny dot at the point where the seam lines intersect.

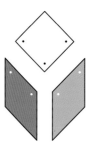

Curved Seams

Some blocks have curved pieces that require special handling. One piece has a concave curve and the other a convex curve.

1. After cutting the pieces, using the appropriate templates, mark the center points on each piece for matching purposes.

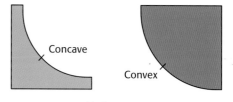

Concave

Convex

Mark centers.

2. To make the concave curve fit the convex curve, make ⅛"-deep clips into the seam allowance of the concave curve. Make only a few clips at first; make more later if needed.

Center

Make ⅛" deep clips.

3. Pin the concave piece to the convex curve with centers matching, using plenty of pins and making additional clips in the concave piece only if necessary. Stitch. Press the seam toward the convex piece.

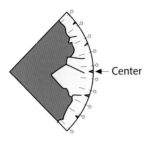

← Center

Paper Piecing

1. Trace and cut out the paper pattern for the block you will be making. Cut it out outside the line—you will trim the fabrics to leave an exact ¼" seam allowance on the paper pattern after the stitching of each section is completed.

2. Cut fabric pieces or strips approximately ¾" wider and ¾" longer than the patch you will be sewing.

3. Place the first fabric piece right side up on the side of the pattern without any lines on it. Hold the paper up to the light to make sure that the fabric piece extends over the edges of the shape by at least ¼" inch all around. Grain line is not as important in this method as in traditional piecing, as the paper gives the block stability while you are sewing.

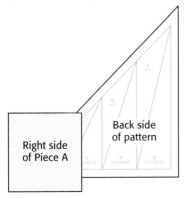

Right side of Piece A

Back side of pattern

4. Place the second fabric piece right sides together with the first fabric piece. Hold them up to the light to make sure that you have left ample fabric on all sides to cover the B shape plus at least ¼" seam allowances.

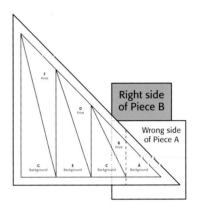

Right side of Piece B

Wrong side of Piece A

5. Use a #90 sewing machine needle (this larger needle perforates the paper better), a sewing thread to blend, and a smaller-than-usual stitch length (approximately 10 to 12 stitches per inch—use your judgment; you want the paper to be easy to tear away but you don't want your stitch so small that it is difficult to rip out if you make a mistake).

6. Start sewing 1 or 2 stitches before the line and continue 1 or 2 stitches past the line so that the seam will be secure.

7. Open up the patches and press.

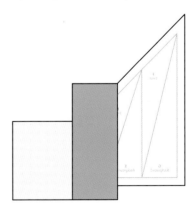

8. Fold the paper pattern back and trim the seam to a scant ¼" or less.

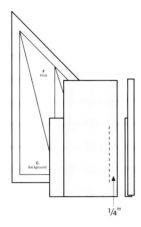

9. Continue in this manner in order until the pattern is completely covered with fabric pieces.

10. Use scissors or a rotary cutter to trim away the excess fabric around the block, leaving a ¼" seam allowance all around.

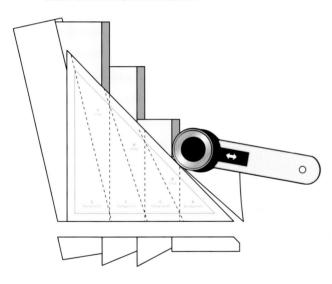

11. Leave the paper on the back side of your work until after you join the completed units to make the block. Then carefully tear away the paper. For more detailed directions on paper piecing, see *Show Me How to Paper Piece* by Carol Doak (That Patchwork Place, 1997).

Mitered Borders

Mitered corners are particularly attractive when using a striped fabric for a border. Blocks sometimes have borders and they can be mitered, too.

Before cutting the striped borders, you may want to experiment with the fabric by folding it at 45° angles in several places to find an area that will form a pleasing design when mitered at the corner. You can also use hinged mirrors placed along the stripe in different places to see what the design will look like when mitered. Cut all striped pieces exactly the same so that the design formed will be the same at each corner.

If the motif in a striped design is directional, you can cut each border strip in two pieces, then join them carefully so the pattern matches at the center of each strip, creating a border with a two-way design.

Design reverses at joining seam.

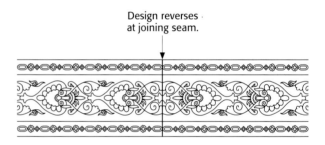

When using a stripe for the borders, sew the borders onto the quilt separately so that you can more easily control the stripes. The design formed at each corner should be the same. If a block, such as the Tree of Life medallion in the center of this quilt, has a border, measure the block for the correct border lengths and attach the border strips as described below. Although the diagrams show how to measure and add the first border, the process is the same for each of the borders in this quilt.

1. As you add each border, determine the finished outside dimensions of the quilt top after adding that border (as indicated by the arrows at the outside edges of the diagram). Add about 4" to this measurement for seam allowances and ease of matching. Trim the border strips to this measurement.

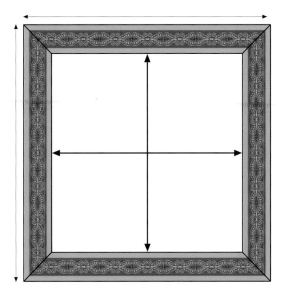

Add 4" to the outside dimensions, including borders.

2. Measure the width and length of the quilt top through the center, seam line to seam line, not including seam allowances (as indicated by the arrows in the center of the quilt in the diagram above).

3. Pin-mark each border strip as shown, placing a pin at the center and one at each end to mark the length of the quilt side.

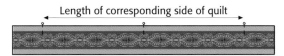

Length of corresponding side of quilt

4. Pin a border strip to the corresponding edge of the quilt top, matching the center and corners. The border design should be exactly the same at each corner; the border strip should extend exactly the same length beyond the quilt edge at both corners. Pin generously. If necessary, ease or stretch to fit. A little steam pressing can be helpful when adjusting borders to fit the outer edges of the quilt.

5. Begin stitching the border to the quilt top exactly ¼" in from one corner and stop exactly ¼" from the other end. Backstitch.

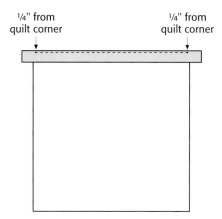

¼" from quilt corner   ¼" from quilt corner

Pin and stitch the remaining three border strips to the quilt top in the same manner.

6. Arrange one corner of the quilt, right side up, on the ironing board. Fold one border strip under at a 45° angle to the other strip. Work with each strip in the border so that each corner forms the same design and miters perfectly.

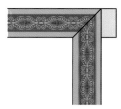

Fold border strip under at a 45° angle.

7. Pin the fold, pointing all pins from the quilt center outward. Press a crease in the fold. Use a ruler to make sure that the corner is square and that the diagonal line from the inner to the outer corner is a true 45° angle.

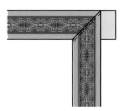

Pin fold with pins pointing outward.

8. Center 1"-wide masking tape over the mitered corner, beginning at the outer edge of the border and removing pins as you work toward the quilt center.

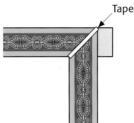

Remove pins as you
tape corner.

9. Turn the quilt over, fold diagonally, and draw a light pencil line on the crease created by the pressing in step 7.

10. Stitch on the pencil line and remove the tape.

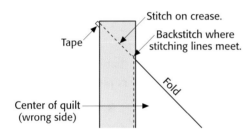

Stitch on crease.
Backstitch where
stitching lines meet.
Tape
Fold
Center of quilt
(wrong side)

Tip

Use a basting stitch on the sewing machine to stitch the miter. After stitching, remove the masking tape on the right side and examine each mitered corner to make sure the stripes within the border match. If not, remove stitches where needed, then tape and restitch the seam in the unstitched areas. Check again. When you are satisfied with the match, change to a regular stitch length and stitch. Remove the basting stitches.

---

11. Trim away excess border length, leaving a ¼"-wide seam allowance; press the seam open.

12. Repeat steps 6–11 on the remaining corners.

13. Attach all remaining borders in the same manner.

Binding

The binding strips for the projects in this book are cut 2¼" wide on the straight grain of the fabric. Join the binding strips end to end until the binding is long enough to go around the perimeter of the quilt plus 10" more, to allow for mitering the corners. Then follow these steps to attach the binding to your quilt.

1. Fold the binding in half, wrong sides together, and press it to make a double-fold binding that is 1⅛" wide. It is easier to sew the binding onto the quilt before trimming the quilt batting and backing; you can hold onto the fabric more easily, and puckers will be less likely to form on the back side of the quilt.

2. Start sewing the binding onto the quilt somewhere along one side, leaving a 2" tail of binding free when you start. Use a walking foot and sew a ¼" seam through all the layers of the quilt. Keep the raw edges of the binding even with the raw edge of the quilt top. Stop sewing exactly ¼" from the next corner of the quilt, backstitch, and cut the thread. Fold the binding up so that the raw edges are in line with the raw edges of the next side of the quilt.

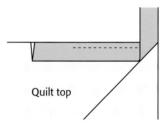

Quilt top

Tip

If the quilt has a mitered border, make sure the diagonal fold on the binding lines up with the mitered corner seam on the border.

---

3. Fold the binding back down on itself, even with the edge of the quilt top, this forms a little pleat at the corner, which later forms the miter at the corner. Begin stitching ¼" in from the edge, backstitching to secure. Repeat this process at each corner of the quilt, and continue stitching until you are about 3" from where you started.

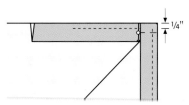

4. Stop stitching, and remove the quilt from your sewing machine. Fold the binding strips together where they should meet, and mark with a pencil.

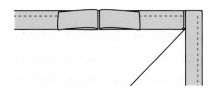

Mark where strips meet.

5. Sew a joining seam on the line you marked. Trim the seam to ¼" and finger-press it open. Put the quilt back in your machine, and sew the remainder of the binding seam.

6. Trim the excess batting and backing even with the edge of the quilt top.

7. Fold the binding over the raw edges of the quilt. Hand sew the fold of the binding onto the back of the quilt so that the fold just covers the previous row of machine stitching. Fold the miter at each corner of the binding by hand, and slipstitch in place.

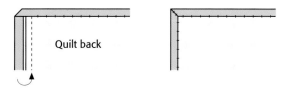

Quilt back

Quilt Plan

Finished Size: 90" x 90"

Materials: 44"-wide fabric

4 yds. ecru for background

3 yds. green print for setting
pieces and blocks

2 yds. dark blue print for blocks

5½ yds. striped fabric for borders*

1 yd. medium blue print for blocks

8 yds. for backing (or 3 yds. of 108"-wide fabric)

¼ yd. navy blue tone-on-tone print

⅔ yd. green print for binding

95" x 95" square of batting

*The amount required depends on the number of repeats of the same stripe across the fabric width. See "Fabric Selection" on page 5.

Cutting Alert

Read this before you cut!

Before cutting any pieces for the individual blocks, cut the border pieces. Cut striped border pieces along the lengthwise grain, adding ¼"-wide seam allowances on both sides of the stripe. Plan borders carefully. Identify a 4½"-wide (finished) design area for the border that surrounds the completed central medallion (Border #2) and for the outermost border (Border #5). You will need to identify another design area that measures 2¾" wide (finished) for the border that surrounds the Tree of Life block (Border #1) and the border that surrounds the blocks and the setting pieces (Border #3). Label the border pieces, and set them aside.

Cutting the Borders

The lengths given for the border strips are longer than required. You will trim them to the correct size as you add them to the growing quilt top.

From the ecru background fabric, cut:
8 strips, each 6½" wide, cutting across the fabric width (crosswise grain). Set these aside for Border #4 (appliquéd border).

From the green print, cut:
6 squares, each 14" x 14", cut twice diagonally for 24 large side setting triangles.

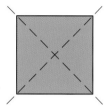

8 squares, each 7¼" x 7¼"; cut in half diagonally to yield 4 corner setting triangles and 12 small side setting triangles.

From the dark blue print, cut:
2 squares, each 12½" x 12½"; cut in half diagonally to yield 4 corner triangles for the medallion.

From the striped fabric, cut the following lengthwise strips:

Border #5 (See Cutting Note on page 23.)
4 strips, each 5" x 96",
OR 8 strips, each 5" x 48"

Border #2 (See Cutting Note on page 23.)
8 strips, each 5" x 26"

Border #1 (See Cutting Note at right.)
4 strips, each 3¼" x 28",
OR 8 strips, each 3¼" x 14"

Border #3 (See Cutting Note at right.)
4 strips, each 3¼" x 72",
OR 8 strips, each 3¼" x 36"

Cutting Note

If the design is one way and you want it to reverse direction at the center so the design meets in the quilt corners, cut 8 strips that are identical in the location of the design motifs within the stripe. This method requires careful piecing to match the design.

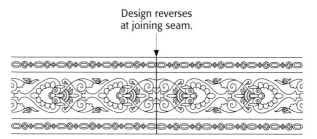

Design reverses
at joining seam.

Tip

If you cannot find fabric with stripes that are the same width as those used in Patricia's quilt, you can easily find the size to cut the 4 corner triangles for the medallion of your quilt by drafting one-quarter of the center medallion, using the width of the stripes on your own fabric as shown:

1. Draw a square that measures 19⅛" x 19⅛" on a 20" square (or larger) piece of ¼" graph paper.

2. Measure over 14" from the left-hand corner in both directions; draw a diagonal line. This diagonal line should be 20" long, which is the finished measurement of one side of the Tree of Life block.

3. Add Border #1 by measuring the finished width of your stripe and drawing another diagonal line parallel to the first.

4. Measure the finished width of the strip you wish to use in Border #2. On the graph paper, draw in the lines of Border #2, adding a diagonal line to indicate the mitered corner.

5. Measure the corner triangle, and add ¼" on all sides for seam allowances to make your template.

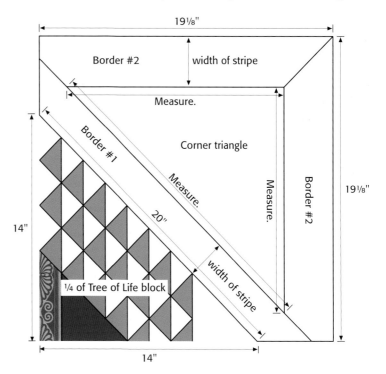

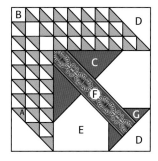

Finished block: 20" x 20"
Finished medallion: 38¼" x 38¼"

And out of the ground the Lord God made to grow every tree that is pleasant to the sight and good for food, the tree of life also in the midst of the garden, and the tree of the knowledge of good and evil.

Genesis 2:9

Cutting

All measurements include ¼"-wide seam allowances. Use Templates #1 and #2 on pages 65–67. See the general directions for cutting pieces from striped fabric on page 13. You will need a 6" or 8" Bias Square® ruler to cut the required bias-square units. These rulers are available at most quilt shops, or see mail-order information on the product page at the end of this book.

A Triangles and Bias-Square Units

1. Cut 3 squares, each 2⅞" x 2⅞", from green print. Cut in half diagonally to yield 6 half-square A triangles for the ends of the tree, next to the D pieces.

2. Cut 2 squares, each 12" x 12", from green print, and 2 from ecru background fabric. Pair a green square and an ecru square right sides together. Repeat with the remaining 2 green and ecru squares. Stack the squares and cut into 2½"-wide bias strips.

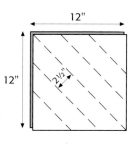

Make 2 sets.

3. Sew each green bias strip to an ecru bias strip along one long edge. Press the seam toward the green strip.

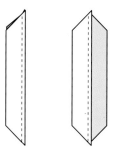

24

4. Using the Bias Square ruler, cut 36 bias-square units as follows:

To cut bias squares:

Position the square at the point of the strip-pieced unit with the diagonal on the seam line and the 2⅝" marks on the bottom edges. Make 2 cuts to separate the square from the unit. Then turn the cut piece around, position the Bias Square for a 2½" square, and cut the remaining 2 edges. Continue cutting 2½" bias-square units from the strip-pieced units until you have 36. You will have leftover green and tan triangles to save for another project.

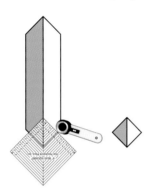

Cut 2⅝" square.

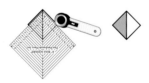

Trim to 2½" square.

Piece B
Cut 3 squares, each 2½" x 2½", from ecru background fabric.

Piece C
Cut 1 square, 6½" x 6½", from dark blue print; cut in half diagonally to yield 2 half-square triangles.

Piece D
Cut 2 squares, each 6⅞" x 6⅞", from ecru background fabric; cut in half diagonally to yield 4 half-square triangles. You need only 3 for the block.

Piece E
Cut 2 Template #1 from ecru background fabric.

Piece F
Cut 1 Template #2 from striped fabric, positioning the grain-line arrow parallel to the stripe.

Piece G
Cut 1 square, 3¾" x 3¾", from dark blue print; cut in half diagonally to yield 2 half-square triangles.

Directions

1. Join the green/ecru bias squares with the green half-square triangles (Piece A) and the ecru squares (Piece B) to complete 2 treetop units as shown.

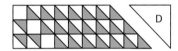

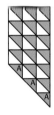

2. Add the ecru half-square triangle (Piece D) to one end of each completed unit.

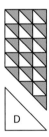

3. Sew 1 half-square triangle (Piece C) and 1 half-square triangle (Piece G) to each ecru background Piece E. Make 1 and 1 reversed.

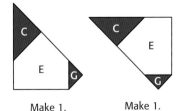

Make 1.   Make 1.

4. Add the completed C/E/G units to each side of Piece F (tree trunk). Sew the remaining Piece D to the base of the tree trunk unit.

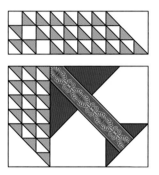

Tree trunk unit

5. Sew the smaller treetop unit to the tree trunk unit first, then add the larger one to complete the block.

6. Add the 3¼"-wide strips for Border #1 to the Tree of Life block, measuring and stitching as described for "Mitered Borders" on pages 17–19.

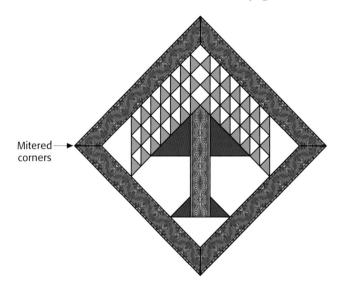

Mitered → corners

7. Sew a 5" x 26" strip for Border #2 to each short side of the dark blue corner triangles, being careful to position them so the design motif is in the same position at the corners. Miter the corners as shown on pages 17–19. Border strips will extend beyond the ends of the triangles. Being careful not to stretch the edge, pin-mark the center of the long edge of the triangles.

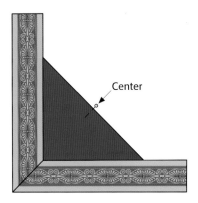

Center

8. Pin-mark the center point on each side of Border #1 on the completed Tree of Life block.

9. Matching center marks, pin and stitch a corner triangle to each side of the Tree of Life block. Begin and end stitching exactly at the seam intersections as shown. Backstitch. The border strips will extend beyond the edges of the block.

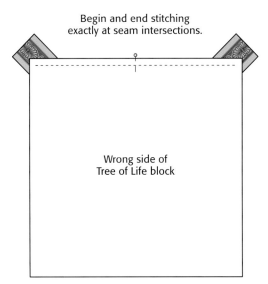

Begin and end stitching
exactly at seam intersections.

Wrong side of
Tree of Life block

10. Fold the block in half and sew the 2 border strips together on opposite sides of the block, backstitching where the stitching meets the seam stitched in step 9. Cut away the excess border fabric, leaving a ¼"-wide seam allowance. Press seams open. Repeat with the remaining 2 sides of the block. The Tree of Life block will extend into Border #2 on all 4 sides.

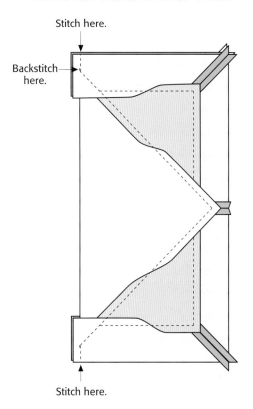

Stitch here.

Backstitch here.

Stitch here.

CHILDREN OF ISRAEL

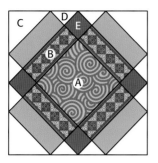

Children of Israel
Finished size: 9"

The Lord said to Moses, "Why do you cry to me? Tell the people of Israel to go forward. Lift up your rod, and stretch out your hand over the sea and divide it, that the people of Israel may go on dry ground through the sea."

Exodus 14:15–16

Cutting

All measurements include ¼"-wide seam allowances. Use Children of Israel Templates #21, #24, #30, and #31 on pages 69–70. See the general directions for cutting striped fabric on page 13.

Piece A

Cut 1 Template #30 from medium blue print.

Piece B

1. Cut 4 Template #24 from striped fabric, positioning the grain-line arrow parallel to the stripe.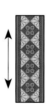

2. Cut 4 Template #24 from green print.

Piece C

Cut 4 Template #31 from ecru background fabric.

Piece D

Cut 8 Template #21 from ecru background fabric.

Piece E

Cut 4 squares, each 1¾" x 1¾", from dark blue print.

Directions

1. Sew 1 ecru background Piece D to each end of a green Piece B. Add Piece C.

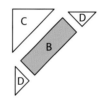

Make 2.

2. Sew 2 Piece D and 2 Piece E to striped Piece B as shown.

Make 2.

3. Add a completed unit to each corner unit.

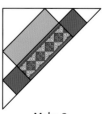

Make 2.

4. Assemble the center unit, using the remaining cut pieces as shown.

5. Sew the units together to complete the block.

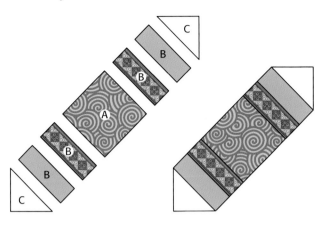

CROSS AND CROWN

Cross and Crown
Finished size: 9"

"So I'll cherish the old rugged Cross,
Till my trophies at last I lay down.
I will cling to the old rugged Cross,
And exchange it some day for a crown."
　　　　　　Hymn by Rev. George Bennard

Be faithful unto death, and I will give you the crown of life.
　　　　　　　　　　　Revelation 2:10

Cutting

All measurements include ¼"-wide seam allowances. Use Cross and Crown Templates #18–#22 on page 69. See general directions for cutting striped fabric on page 13.

Piece A
Cut 4 Template #22 from ecru background fabric.
Cut 1 Template #22 from dark blue print.

Piece B
Cut 4 Template #18 from striped fabric, positioning the grain-line arrow parallel to the stripe.

Piece C
Cut 4 Template #20 from medium blue print.

Piece D

Cut 1 Template #19 from striped fabric, positioning the grain-line arrow parallel to the stripe.

Piece E

Cut 8 Template #21 from dark blue print and 8 from ecru background fabric.

Directions

1. Sew l dark blue triangle (Piece E) to 1 ecru background triangle (Piece E). Make 4 of each unit.

Make 4.   Make 4.

2. Sew 1 E/E unit to each side of ecru background Piece A. Make 4.

Make 4.

3. Sew 1 medium blue Piece C to striped Piece D. Sew the A/E/E and C/D units together. Make 4.

Make 4.

4. Sew a striped Piece B to opposite sides of a dark blue Piece A.

5. Add the remaining striped B pieces between the step 3 units to make 2 rows as shown.

Make 2.

6. Join the vertical rows to complete the block.

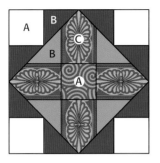

Cross within a Cross
Finished size: 9"

And as they led him away, they seized one Simon of Cyre'ne, who was coming in from the country, and laid on him the cross, to carry it behind Jesus.

Luke 23:26

Cutting

All measurements include ¼"-wide seam allowances. Use Cross within a Cross Template #6 on page 67. See general directions for cutting striped fabrics on page 13.

Piece A

1. Cut 4 squares, each 2¾" x 2¾", from ecru background fabric.

2. Cut 1 square, 2¾" x 2¾", from medium blue print.

Piece B

1. Cut 4 squares, each 3⅛" x 3⅛", from dark blue print; cut in half diagonally to yield 8 half-square triangles.

2. Cut 2 squares, each 3⅛" x 3⅛", from green print; cut in half diagonally to yield 4 half-square triangles.

Piece C

Cut 4 Template #6 from striped fabric, positioning the grain-line arrow parallel to the stripe.

Directions

1. Sew a green Piece B to each side of a striped Piece C to make a pieced triangle for the center unit. Make 2. Sew the remaining 2 Piece C to medium blue print Piece A. Sew the completed units together to complete the center unit.

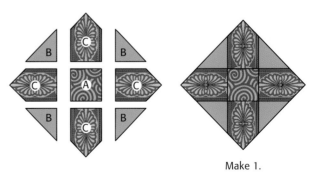

Make 1.

2. Sew 1 dark blue Piece B to each side of an ecru background square (Piece A) for a corner unit.

Make 4.

3. Join a corner unit to opposite sides of the center unit. Repeat with remaining corner units to complete the block.

CROWN OF THORNS

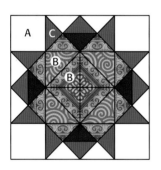

Crown of Thorns
Finished size: 9"

And they clothed him in a purple cloak, and plaiting a crown of thorns they put it on him. And they began to salute him, "Hail, King of the Jews!"

Mark 15:17–18

Cutting

All measurements include ¼"-wide seam allowances. Use Crown of Thorns Templates #13 and #14 on page 68. See general directions for cutting striped fabric on page 13.

Piece A

Cut 4 squares, each 2¾" x 2¾", from ecru background fabric.

Piece B

1. Cut 2 squares, each 3⅛" x 3⅛", from medium blue print; cut in half diagonally to yield 4 half-square triangles, or use Template #13 and cut 4 if you have a design you wish to center.

2. Cut 4 Template #13 from striped fabric, positioning the grain-line arrow parallel to the stripe.

Piece C

1. Cut 2 squares, each 3½" x 3½", from ecru background fabric.
2. Cut 1 square, 3½" x 3½", from navy print.
3. Cut 3 squares, each 3½" x 3½", from dark blue print.
4. Stack the squares and cut twice diagonally to yield 8 ecru background, 4 navy print, and 12 dark blue print quarter-square triangles.

5. Cut 8 Template #14 from striped fabric, positioning the grain-line arrow parallel to the stripe.

Directions

1. Sew 4 striped Piece B together for center of block as shown.

2. Sew 1 medium blue Piece B to opposite sides of the square unit. Repeat with the remaining 2 medium blue triangles.

3. Using the dark blue, navy, ecru, and striped triangles (Piece C), make 4 units, following the piecing diagram.

Make 4.

4. Sew the completed units together in 3 vertical rows, adding Piece A where shown.

5. Join the vertical rows to complete the block.

DAVID AND GOLIATH

David and Goliath
Finished size: 9"

And there came out from the camp of the Philistines a champion named Goliath, of Gath, whose height was six cubits and a span. . . . And David put his hand in his bag and took out a stone, and slung it, and struck the Philistine on his forehead; the stone sank into his forehead, and he fell on his face to the ground.

I Samuel 17:4, 49

Cutting

All measurements include ¼"-wide seam allowances. Use David and Goliath Templates #20–#23 on page 69. See the general directions for cutting striped fabric on page 13.

Piece A

1. Cut 8 Template #22 from ecru background fabric.

2. Cut 1 Template #22 from dark blue print.

3. Cut 4 Template #22 from striped fabric, positioning the grain-line arrow parallel to the stripe.

Piece B

Cut 4 Template #20 from striped fabric, positioning carefully so the stripes will line up where they join Piece A at the edges nearest the outside of the block.

Piece C

Cut 8 Template #21 from ecru background fabric.

Piece D

1. Cut 4 Template #23 and 4 Template #23 reversed from striped fabric, positioning the grain-line arrow parallel to the stripe.

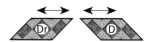

2. Cut 4 Template #23 and 4 Template #23 reversed from dark blue print.

Directions

1. Sew Piece D together in pairs, making 4 chevron units with the stripe on the left and 4 with the stripe on the right. Stitch in the direction of the arrow, ending stitching ¼" from the raw edge. Backstitch.

Make 4.   Make 4.

2. Sew chevrons together in pairs. Stitch in the direction of the arrow, ending stitching ¼" from the raw edge at the inside corner. Backstitch.

Make 4.

3. Referring to "Set-in-Seams" on page 15, add 1 Piece A and 2 Piece C to each chevron unit, stitching in the direction of the arrows.

4. Sew Piece B to each chevron unit to complete 4 corner units.

Make 4.

5. Sew each striped Piece A to an ecru background Piece A to make 4 bar units.

Make 4.

6. Assemble the block in 3 vertical rows, using the completed corner and bar units and the remaining dark blue Piece A.

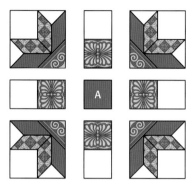

7. Join the vertical rows to complete the block.

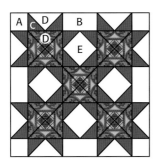

Devil's Claws
Finished size: 9"

Be sober, be watchful. Your adversary the devil prowls around like a roaring lion, seeking someone to devour. Resist him, firm in your faith, knowing that the same experience of suffering is required of your brotherhood throughout the world. And after you have suffered a little while, the God of all grace, who has called you to his eternal glory in Christ, will himself restore, establish, and strengthen you.

I Peter 5:8–10

Cutting

All measurements include ¼"-wide seam allowances. Use Devil's Claws Template #4 on page 67. See the general directions for cutting striped fabric on page 13.

Pieces A and B

Cut 1 strip, 1⅝" x 20", from ecru background fabric; crosscut into 4 squares, each 1⅝" x 1⅝", for Piece A, and 4 rectangles, each 1⅝" x 2¾", for Piece B.

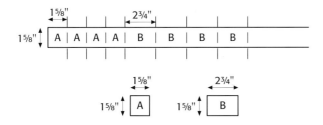

Piece C

Cut 1 strip, 2" x 42", from dark blue print; crosscut into 16 squares, each 2" x 2". Stack squares and cut in half diagonally to yield 32 half-square triangles.

Piece D

1. Cut 2 squares, each 3½" x 3½", from ecru back-ground fabric; cut twice diagonally to yield 8 quarter-square triangles.

2. Cut 20 Template #4 from striped fabric, positioning the grain-line arrow parallel to the stripe.

Piece E

Cut 4 squares, each 2⅛" x 2⅛", from ecru back-ground fabric.

Directions

1. Sew striped triangles (Piece D) together in pairs along the short sides. Join pairs to make 5 squares as shown.

Make 10.

Make 5.

2. Sew 1 dark blue triangle (Piece C) to each side of an ecru background triangle (Piece D). Make 8.

Make 8.

3. Sew remaining dark blue triangles (Piece C) to opposite sides of each ecru background square (Piece E), then to the remaining 2 sides as shown. Make 4.

Make 4.

4. Sew the completed units together in 5 vertical rows. Press the seams toward the C pieces.

5. Join the vertical rows to complete the block.

DEVIL'S PUZZLE (ALTERNATE BLOCK)

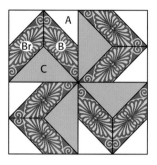

Devil's Puzzle
Finished size: 9"

Finally, be strong in the Lord and in the strength of his might. Put on the whole armor of God, that you may be able to stand against the wiles of the devil.

Ephesians 6:10–11

Cutting

All measurements include ¼"-wide seam allowances. Use Devil's Puzzle Template #5 on page 67. See general directions for cutting striped fabric on page 13.

Piece A

Cut 4 squares, each 3⅛" x 3⅛", from ecru background fabric; cut squares in half diagonally to yield 8 half-square triangles.

Piece B

Cut 4 each of Template #5 and Template #5 reversed from striped fabric, positioning the grainline arrow parallel to the stripe.

Piece C

Cut 1 square, 5¾" x 5¾", from green print fabric; cut twice diagonally to yield 4 quarter-square triangles.

Directions

1. Sew 1 ecru background triangle (Piece A) to 1 striped Piece B as shown. Make 4. Repeat with the pieces reversed.

Make 4.

Make 4.

2. Sew units together in pairs, stitching in the direction of the arrow and ending the stitching ¼" from the inside corner. Backstitch. Trim away points at outer edge. Make 4.

Make 4.

3. Referring to "Set-in-Seams" on page 15, sew each completed unit to a green print triangle (Piece C). Match the seam intersection at the point of the green triangle to the seam inter-section at the inside corner of the unit. Pin in place. Stitch from the inside edge to the outer corner, sewing as close to the beginning corner pin as possible without sewing past it. Backstitch. Attach the second side of the triangle in the same manner.

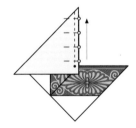

Make 4.

4. Sew the completed units together in 2 vertical rows.

5. Join the vertical rows to complete the block.

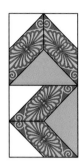

GARDEN OF EDEN

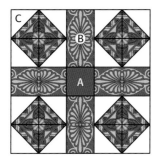

Garden of Eden
Finished size: 9"

*And the Lord God planted a garden in Eden, in the east;
and there he put the man whom he had formed.*

Genesis 2:8

Cutting

All measurements include ¼"-wide seam allowances. Use
Garden of Eden Templates #18, #20, and #22 on page 69. See the
general directions for cutting striped fabric on page 13.

Piece A

Cut 1 Template #22 from dark blue print.

Piece B

Cut 4 Template #18 from striped fabric, positioning
the grain-line arrow parallel to the stripe.

Piece C

1. Cut 16 Template #20 from ecru background
   fabric. Position the short sides of the template
   along the straight grain.

2. Cut 16 Template #20 from striped fabric,
   positioning the longest edge parallel to the
   stripe.

Directions

1. Sew 4 striped Piece C together as shown to
   make the center for each of the 4 corner units.

Make 4.

2. Sew 1 ecru background Piece C to opposite
   sides of each center and then to the remaining
   two sides to complete 4 corner units.

Make 4.

3. Using the corner units and the remaining cut
   pieces, assemble the block in 3 vertical rows as
   shown. Press the seams toward the B pieces.

4. Sew rows together to complete the block.

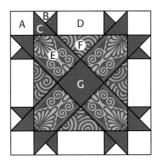

Golgotha
Finished size: 9"

And they brought him to the place called Gol'gotha (which means the place of a skull). And they offered him wine mingled with myrrh; but he did not take it. And they crucified him, and divided his garments among them, casting lots for them, to decide what each should take.

Mark 15:22–24

Cutting

All measurements include ¼"-wide seam allowances. Use Golgotha Templates #15 and #16 on pages 68–69. See general directions for cutting striped fabric on page 13.

Piece A

Cut 4 squares, each 2" x 2", from ecru background fabric.

Piece B

Cut 2 squares, each 2¾" x 2¾", from ecru background fabric and 2 from dark blue print. Stack squares and cut twice diagonally to yield 8 quarter-square triangles from each fabric.

Piece C

Cut 4 squares, each 2⅜" x 2⅜", from dark blue print. Stack squares and cut in half diagonally to yield 8 half-square triangles.

Piece D

Cut 4 rectangles, each 2" x 3½", from ecru background fabric.

Piece E

Cut 4 Template #15 from striped fabric, positioning the grain-line arrow parallel to the stripe.

Piece F

Cut 1 square, 4¼" x 4¼", from medium blue print; cut twice diagonally to yield 4 quarter-square triangles or use Template #16 and cut 4 if you wish to center a design.

Piece G

Cut 1 square, 2⅝" x 2⅝", from dark blue print.

Directions

1. Assemble the center unit as shown, using Pieces E, F, and G.

2. Sew each ecru background Piece B to a dark blue Piece B, making 2 sets of mirror-image units.

Make 4. Make 4.

Sew these units to Piece C. Make 4 of each unit as shown.

Make 4. Make 4.

3. Sew completed C/B/B units to opposite ends of each Piece D, paying careful attention to placement. Make 4.

Make 4.

Sew 1 of these units to the top and 1 to the bottom edge of the center unit.

4. Sew an ecru background square (Piece A) to each end of the remaining 2 units.

5. Sew a unit made in step 4 to each side of the center unit to complete the block.

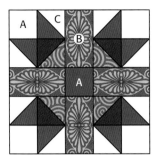

Heavenly Problems
Finished size: 9"

Now war arose in heaven, Michael and his angels fighting against the dragon; and the dragon and his angels fought, but they were defeated and there was no longer any place for them in heaven. And the great dragon was thrown down, that ancient serpent, who is called the Devil and Satan, the deceiver of the whole world—he was thrown down to the earth, and his angels were thrown down with him.

Revelation 12:7–9

Cutting

All measurements include ¼"-wide seam allowances. Use Heavenly Problems Templates #18, #20, and #22 on page 69. See the general directions for cutting striped fabric on page 13.

Piece A
1. Cut 4 Template #22 from ecru background fabric.
2. Cut 1 Template #22 from dark blue print.

Piece B
Cut 4 Template #18 from striped fabric, positioning the grain-line arrow parallel to the stripe.

Piece C
1. Cut 8 Template #20 from dark blue print and 8 from ecru background fabric.
2. Cut 4 Template #20 from medium blue print and 4 from navy print.

Directions

1. Sew each ecru background Piece C to 1 dark blue Piece C to make 8 bias-square units.

   Make 8.

2. Sew each medium blue Piece C to 1 navy Piece C to make 4 bias-square units.

   Make 4.

3. Sew bias-square units and ecru background squares (Piece A) together in vertical rows as shown. Join the rows to make 4 corner units.

   Make 4.

4. Using the completed corner units and the remaining cut pieces, assemble the pieces in 3 vertical rows as shown, then sew the rows together to complete the block.

Heavenly Stars

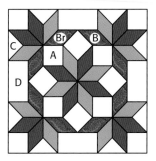

Heavenly Stars
Finished size: 9"

For we know that if the earthly tent we live in is destroyed, we have a building from God, a house not made with hands, eternal in the heavens.

2 Corinthians 5:1

Cutting

All measurements include ¼"-wide seam allowances. Use Heavenly Stars Templates #25, #28, and #29 on page 70. See the general directions for cutting striped fabric on page 13.

Piece A
Cut 12 Template #28 from ecru background fabric.

Piece B
Cut 12 Template #25 from dark blue print, 12 from green print, and 4 and 4 reversed from striped fabric, positioning the grain-line arrow parallel to the stripe.

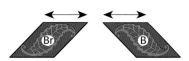

Piece C
Cut 2 squares, each 3⅛" x 3⅛", from ecru background fabric. Stack squares and cut twice diagonally to yield 8 quarter-square triangles.

Piece D
Cut 4 Template #29 from ecru background fabric.

Directions

1. To make the center star, make 4 chevron units, using the dark blue and green diamonds (Piece B). Stitch in the direction of the arrow, ending stitching ¼" from the raw edge as shown. Backstitch. Press all seams toward the dark blue diamonds.

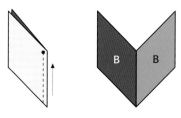

2. To make a half-star unit, sew the chevrons together in 2 pairs, stitching in the direction of the arrow and ending the stitching ¼" from the raw edge. Backstitch. Press seams toward the dark blue diamonds.

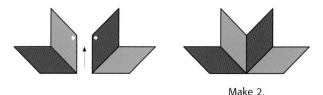

Make 2.

3. Join the half-star units to complete the star, beginning and ending the stitching ¼" from each raw edge as indicated by the dots in the diagram. Backstitch.

Begin and end stitching at dots.

4. Referring to "Set-in Seams" on page 15, add Piece A between each set of star points, stitching in the direction of the arrows. Begin and end stitching ¼" from the raw edges at both the inner corner and outer point as indicated by the dots in the square. Backstitch.

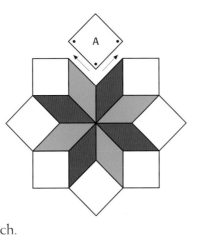

5. In the same manner, attach a striped diamond to adjacent squares, stitching from the center dot to the point on each half as indicated by the arrows.

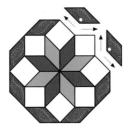

6. For the corner units, assemble 2 mirror-image sets of chevrons as shown, using the remaining diamonds (Piece B). Make 4 of each set. Stitch as shown in step 1.

Make 4.   Make 4.

7. Sew chevron sets together in 4 pairs as shown in step 2.

Make 4.

8. Add an ecru background Piece A and 2 ecru background Piece C to each corner unit, stitching in the direction of the arrows.

Make 4.

9. Stitch each corner unit to the center star unit. Begin and end stitching ¼" from the raw edges at both ends on each seam. Backstitch.

10. To complete the block, set in 1 Piece D to each side, stitching the long side to the block first and then the short sides. Stitch in the direction of the arrows.

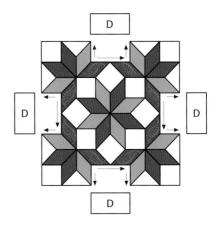

HOSANNA (ALTERNATE BLOCK)

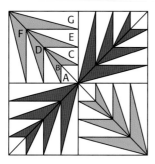

Hosanna
Finished size: 9"

And the crowds that went before him and that followed him shouted, "Hosanna to the Son of David! Blessed is he who comes in the name of the Lord! Hosanna in the highest!

Matthew 21:9

Refer to the directions in "Paper Piecing" on page 16.

1. Copy or trace the foundation patterns on page 71 onto paper. (Make 4 copies of each pattern.)
2. Cut out the patterns outside the lines; you will trim them to the exact size later. You will have 4 and 4 reversed sections.

Cutting

1. Cut fabric strips 2" wide, and cut lengths at least ¾" longer than the piece to be covered.
2. Start piecing with Fabric A, which is the ecru background fabric. Pieces A, C, E, and G will all be from the ecru background fabric.
3. Continue adding fabric strips until the whole section is covered. Pieces B, D, and F will be from green print fabric.
4. Make 2 and 2 reversed sections from green print.

Make 2.   Make 2.

5. Trim exactly on the outside line so that there is a ¼" seam allowance around each section. Baste the sections to make ¼ of the block. Check that the pieces line up exactly; sew. Make 2.

Stitch in direction   Make 2.
of arrow.

6. Repeat steps 1–5, using the dark blue print for Pieces B, D, and F.
7. Sew the quarter blocks together in 2 vertical rows, paying careful attention to the position of Piece A.
8. Join the vertical rows to complete the block.

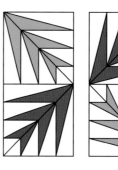

9. Carefully remove the papers.

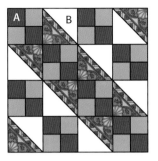

Jacob's Ladder
Finished size: 9"

And he dreamed that there was a ladder set up on the earth, and the top of it reached to heaven; and behold, the angels of God were ascending and descending on it!

Genesis 28:12

Cutting

All measurements include ¼"-wide seam allowances. Use Jacob's Ladder Template #3 on page 67. See the general directions for cutting striped fabric on page 13.

Piece A

1. Cut 1 strip, 1⅝" x 28", from green print.
2. Cut 1 strip, 1⅝" x 28", from dark blue print. Stitch these 2 strips, right sides together, along one long edge. Press seams toward the dark blue print. Cut the strip-pieced unit into 16 segments, each 1⅝" wide. Sew the segments together to make 8 four-patch units.

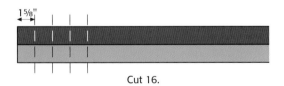

Cut 16.

Make 8.

Piece B

1. Cut 4 squares, each 3⅛" x 3⅛", from ecru background fabric. Stack squares and cut in half diagonally to yield 8 half-square triangles.

2. Cut 8 Template #3 from striped fabric. Position the template in a similar place along the stripe to cut 8 identical triangles. Position the grain-line arrow so it runs parallel to the stripe.

Directions

1. Sew 1 ecru background triangle (Piece B) to 1 striped triangle (Piece B), right sides together. Make 8.

Make 8.

2. Sew units together in 4 vertical rows as shown.

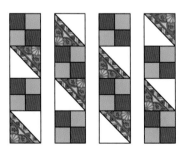

3. Press the seams toward the four-patch units.
4. Join the vertical rows to complete the block.

JOB'S TEARS (ALTERNATE BLOCK)

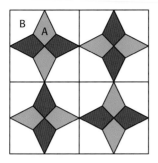

Job's Tears
Finished size: 9"

My friends scorn me; my eye pours out tears to God, that he would maintain the right of a man with God, like that of a man with his neighbor.

Job 16:20–21

Cutting

All measurements include ¼"-wide seam allowances. Use Job's Tears Templates #11 and #12 on page 68.

Piece A

Cut 8 Template #11 from dark blue print and 8 from green print.

Piece B

Cut 16 Template #12 from ecru background fabric.

Note: For matching purposes, mark all seam intersections by making a small hole in the template and marking a dot on the wrong side of the fabric.

Directions

1. Sew each dark blue Piece A to a green Piece A as shown. Begin stitching at the center and stitch to the dot at the seam intersection. Backstitch.

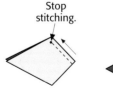

Stop stitching.

Make 8.

2. Sew the completed units together, beginning and ending at the seam-intersection dots. Backstitch at the beginning and ending of the seam, being careful not to stitch past the dots. Make 4.

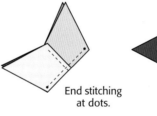

End stitching at dots.

Make 4.

3. Referring to "Set-in Seams" on page 15, sew 4 Piece B to each completed unit, stitching in the direction of the arrows. Backstitch. Make 4.

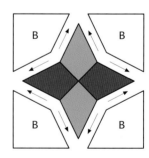

Stitch in direction of arrows.
Make 4.

4. Sew the completed quarter-blocks together in 2 vertical rows.

5. Join the vertical rows to complete the block.

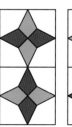

JOSEPH'S COAT

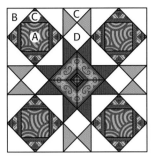

Joseph's Coat
Finished size: 9"

Now Israel loved Joseph more than any other of his children, because he was the son of his old age; and he made him a coat of many colors.

Genesis 37:3

Cutting

All measurements include ¼"-wide seam allowances. Use Joseph's Coat Templates #20–#22 on page 69. See the general directions for cutting striped fabric on page 13.

Piece A

Cut 4 Template #22 from medium blue print.

Piece B

1. Cut 16 Template #20 from ecru background fabric.

2. Cut 4 Template #20 from striped fabric, positioning the longest edge parallel to the stripe.

Piece C

1. Cut 8 Template #21 from dark blue print and 8 from green print.

2. Cut 4 Template #21 from ecru background fabric.

3. Cut 16 Template #21 from striped fabric, positioning the grain-line arrow parallel to the stripe.

Piece D

Cut 4 squares, each 1¾" x 1¾", from ecru background fabric.

Directions

1. Sew together 4 striped Piece B as shown for center unit.

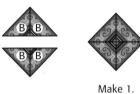

Make 1.

2. Sew 1 dark blue Piece C to each side of an ecru background Piece B.

Make 4.

Sew 1 ecru background Piece D to each end of 2 of these units.

Make 2.

3. Assemble center unit as shown.

49

4. Sew a striped Piece C to opposite sides of a medium blue Piece A. Repeat on remaining sides of the square. Make 4, one for each corner.

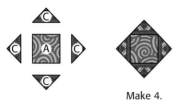

Make 4.

5. Sew 3 ecru background Piece B to each corner unit.

Make 4.

6. Add a green Piece C to opposite sides of these corner units; join 2 of these units to the center unit as shown.

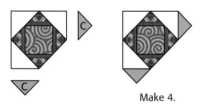

Make 4.

7. Sew 1 ecru background Piece C to each side of the 2 remaining corner units as shown.

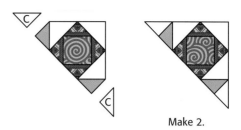

Make 2.

8. Sew the remaining corner units to the center unit to complete the block.

ROAD TO JERUSALEM (ALTERNATE BLOCK)

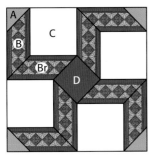

Road to Jerusalem
Finished size: 9"

And when they drew near to Jerusalem . . . they brought the ass and the colt, and put their garments on them, and he sat thereon. Most of the crowd spread their garments on the road, and others cut branches from the trees and spread them on the road.

Matthew 21:1, 7–8

Cutting

All measurements include ¼"-wide seam allowances. Use Road to Jerusalem Template #17 on page 69. See general directions for cutting striped fabric on page 13.

Piece A
Cut 2 squares, each 2⅜" x 2⅜", from green print. Stack squares and cut in half diagonally to yield 4 half-square triangles.

Piece B
Cut 4 Template #17 and 4 Template #17 reversed from striped fabric.

Piece C
Cut 4 squares, each 3½" x 3½", from ecru background fabric.

Piece D
Cut 1 square, 2⅝" x 2⅝", from dark blue print.

Directions

1. Sew each Piece B to a Piece B reversed as shown. Begin stitching from one edge and end ¼" from the other edge. Backstitch carefully.

Stitch in direction of arrow.

2. Referring to "Set-in Seams" on page 15, add Piece C to each unit, stitching in the direction of the arrows. Backstitch. Make 4 corner units.

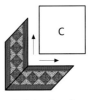

Stitch in direction of arrows.

3. Mark the seam intersections on the wrong side of Piece D at all 4 corners.

51

4. Sew Piece D to 1 corner unit. With D on top, begin and end the stitching at the seam intersection dots. Backstitch.

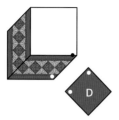

Add the next corner unit in the same manner; then stitch the seam between the two units. Begin at the seam intersection of Piece D and stitch out to the edge of the block in the direction of the arrow.

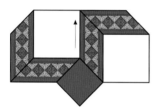

Repeat with the remaining corner units.

5. Add a Piece A to each corner to complete the block.

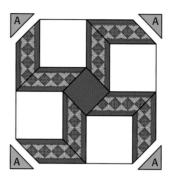

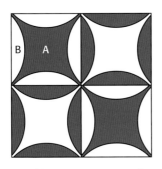

Robbing Peter to Pay Paul
Finished size: 9"

And Peter answered him, "Lord, if it is you, bid me come to you on the water." He said, "Come." So Peter got out of the boat and walked on the water and came to Jesus....

Matthew 14:28–29

And God did extraordinary miracles by the hands of Paul, so that handkerchiefs or aprons were carried away from his body to the sick, and diseases left them and the evil spirits came out of them.

Acts 19:11–12

Cutting

All measurements include ¼"-wide seam allowances. Use Robbing Peter to Pay Paul Templates #9 and #10 on page 68.

Piece A
Cut 2 Template #9 from ecru background fabric and 2 from dark blue print.

Piece B
Cut 8 Template #10 from ecru background fabric and 8 from dark blue print.

Directions

1. Referring to "Curved Seams" on page 15, sew 4 ecru background Piece B to 1 dark blue Piece A. Make 2. Sew 4 dark blue Piece B to 1 ecru background Piece A in the same manner. Make 2.

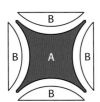

Make 2.

Make 2.

2. Sew completed units together in 2 vertical rows. Press the seams toward the dark blue B pieces.

3. Join the vertical rows to complete the block.

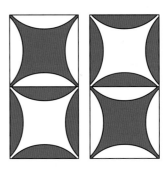

This block is used in Ruth Landon's quilt on page 8.

53

SOLOMON'S PUZZLE

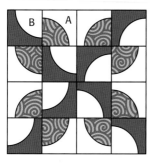

Solomon's Puzzle
Finished size: 9"

And God gave Solomon wisdom and understanding beyond measure, and largeness of mind like the sand on the seashore, so that Solomon's wisdom surpassed the wisdom of all the people of the east, and all the wisdom of Egypt.

I Kings 4:29–30

Cutting

All measurements include ¼"-wide seam allowances. Use Solomon's Puzzle Templates #7 and #8 on page 67.

Piece A
Cut 8 Template #7 from ecru background fabric and 8 from dark blue print.

Piece B
Cut 8 Template #8 from ecru background fabric and 8 from medium blue print.

Directions

1. Sew Pieces A and B together to make 8 dark blue units and 8 medium blue units as shown. See "Curved Seams" on page 15.

Make 8.   Make 8.

2. Sew completed units together in 4 vertical rows, paying careful attention to placement.

3. Join the vertical rows to complete the block.

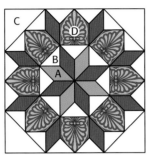

Star of the Magi
Finished size: 9"

Now when Jesus was born in Bethlehem of Judea in the days of Herod the king, behold, wise men from the East came to Jerusalem, saying, "Where is he who has been born king of the Jews? For we have seen his star in the East, and have come to worship him."

Matthew 2:1–2

Cutting

All measurements include ¼"-wide seam allowances. Use Star of the Magi Templates #25 and #27 on page 70. See the general directions for cutting striped fabric on page 13.

Piece A
Cut 12 Template #25 from dark blue print and 4 from green print.

Piece B
Cut 1 strip, 3⅛" x 19", from ecru background fabric; crosscut into 6 squares, each 3⅛" x 3⅛". Stack squares and cut twice diagonally to yield 24 quarter-square triangles.

Piece C
Cut 2 squares, each 3½" x 3½", from ecru background fabric. Stack squares and cut in half diagonally to yield 4 half-square triangles.

Piece D
Cut 8 Template #27 from the striped fabric, positioning the grain-line arrow parallel to the stripe.

Directions

1. To make the center star, make 4 chevron units, using the dark blue and green diamonds (Piece A). Stitch in the direction of the arrow, ending the stitching ¼" from the raw edge as shown. Backstitch. Press all seams toward the dark blue diamonds.

Make 4.

2. To make a half-star unit, sew the chevrons together in 2 pairs, stitching in the direction of the arrow. End the stitching at the dot. Backstitch. Press seams toward the dark blue diamonds.

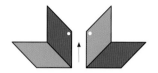

Make 2.

3. Join the half-star units to complete the star, beginning and ending the stitching ¼" from each raw edge as indicated by the dots in the diagram. Backstitch.

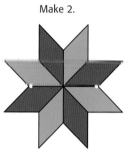

Begin and end stitching at the dots.

4. Referring to "Set-in Seams" on page 15, sew an ecru background triangle (Piece B) between each set of star points. Stitch in the direction of the arrows.

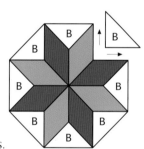

5. Stitch 4 Piece D to the star unit as shown. Stop stitching ¼" in from both ends of the seam. Backstitch.

6. Stitch a dark blue diamond (Piece A) to each side of a Piece D, ending stitching ¼" from the inside corner as shown. Backstitch.

Make 4.

7. Using set-in seams, insert an ecru background triangle (Piece B) between the points of each unit, stitching in the direction of the arrows as shown.

8. Set units into block, stitching in the direction and order of the arrows.

9. Add ecru background triangles (Piece B), stitching in the direction of the arrows as shown.

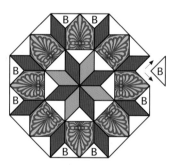

10. Add ecru background triangles (Piece C) to complete the block.

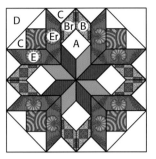

Bethlehem Rose
Finished size: 9"

"And you, O Bethlehem, in the land of Judah, are by no means least among the rulers of Judah; for from you shall come a ruler who will govern my people Israel."

Matthew 2:6

Tip

The Bethlehem Rose block is more challenging than most of the other blocks in this book. You might want to gain experience with easier blocks before starting this one.

Cutting

All measurements include ¼"-wide seam allowances. Use Bethlehem Rose Templates #25, #26, and #28 on page 70. See the general directions for cutting striped fabric on page 13.

Piece A

Cut 4 Template #28 from ecru background fabric and 4 from medium blue print.

Piece B

Use Template #25 to cut 4 dark blue diamonds and 4 green diamonds. Cut 4 and 4 reversed from the striped fabric, positioning the grain-line arrow parallel to the stripe.

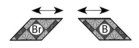

Piece C

Cut 4 squares, each 3⅛" x 3⅛", from ecru background fabric. Stack squares and cut twice diagonally to yield 16 quarter-square triangles.

Piece D

Cut 2 squares, each 3½" x 3½", from ecru background fabric. Stack squares and cut in half diagonally to yield 4 half-square triangles.

Piece E

Use Template #26 to cut 4 and 4 reversed from the striped fabric, positioning the grain-line arrow parallel to the stripe.

Directions

1. To make the center star, make 4 chevron units, using the dark blue and green diamonds (Piece B). Stitch in the direction of the arrow, ending stitching ¼" from the raw edge as shown. Backstitch. Press all seams toward the dark blue diamonds.

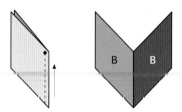

2. To make a half-star unit, sew the chevrons together in 2 pairs, stitching in the direction of the arrow and ending the stitching ¼" from the raw edge. Backstitch. Press the seams toward the dark blue diamonds.

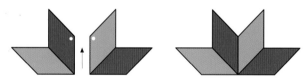

Make 2.

3. Join the half-star units to complete the star, beginning and ending the stitching ¼" from each raw edge as indicated by the dots in the diagram. Backstitch.

Begin and end stitching
at the dots.

4. Referring to "Set-in Seams" on page 15, add Piece A between 4 sets of star points, stitching in the direction of the arrows. Begin and end stitching ¼" from the raw edges at both the inner corner and outer point as indicated by the dots in the square. Backstitch.

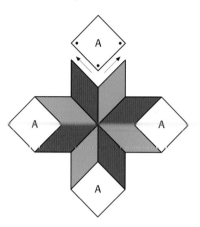

5. Make 4 chevron units, using the striped diamonds (Piece B). Stitch in the direction of the arrow, ending stitching ¼" from the raw edge as shown. Backstitch.

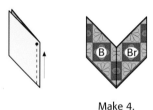

Make 4.

6. Add a striped chevron unit to each square at the outer points of the center star, stitching in the direction of the arrows. Begin and end stitching ¼" from the raw edges at both the inner corner and outer point as indicated by the dots in the square. Backstitch.

7. Make 4 corner units, following the piecing diagram and using medium blue Piece A and ecru background Pieces C and D.

Make 4.

8. Make 4 chevron units, using striped Piece E. Sew as shown in step 5.

Make 4.

9. Add a striped chevron unit to each corner unit, stitching in the direction of the arrows.

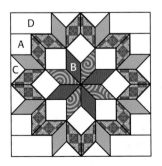

10. Add the corner units to the center star, stitching in the direction of the arrows.

11. Insert remaining ecru background triangles (Piece C) where indicated. Stitch in the direction of the arrows.

CARPENTER'S WHEEL

Carpenter's Wheel
Finished size: 9"

. . . they were astonished, and said, "Where did this man get this wisdom and these mighty works? Is not this the carpenter's son? Is not his mother called Mary?" . . .

Matthew 13:54–55

Cutting

All measurements include ¼"-wide seam allowances. Use Carpenter's Wheel Templates #25, #28, and #29 on page 70. See general directions for cutting striped fabric on page 13.

Piece A

Cut 12 Template #28 from ecru background fabric.

Piece B

Use Template #25 to cut 8 from green print, 4 from dark blue print, 4 from medium blue print, and 8 and 8 reversed from striped fabric, positioning the grain-line arrow parallel to the stripe.

Piece C

Cut 2 squares, each 3⅛" x 3⅛", from ecru background fabric. Stack squares and cut twice diagonally to yield 8 quarter-square triangles.

Piece D

Cut 4 Template #29 from ecru background fabric.

Directions

1. To make the center star, make 4 chevron units, using the dark blue and medium blue diamonds (Piece B). Stitch in the direction of the arrow, ending the stitching ¼" from the raw edge as shown. Backstitch. Press all seams toward the dark blue diamonds.

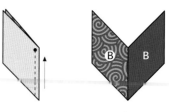

Make 4.

2. To make a half-star unit, sew the chevrons together in 2 pairs, stitching in the direction of the arrows and ending the stitching ¼" from the raw edge. Backstitch. Press seams toward the dark blue diamonds.

Make 2.

3. Join the half-star units to complete the star, beginning and ending the stitching ¼" from each raw edge as indicated by the dots in the diagram. Backstitch.

Begin and end stitching
at the dots.

4. Referring to "Set-in Seams" on page 15, add Piece A between each set of star points, stitching in the direction of the arrows. Begin and end stitching ¼" from the raw edges at both the inner corner and outer point as indicated by the dots in the square. Backstitch.

5. Sew a striped diamond and a reversed striped diamond (Piece B) to each side of a green diamond (Piece B). Stitch in the direction of the arrows and end the stitching ¼" from the raw edge. Backstitch. Make 8 of these star-point units.

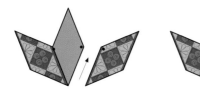

Make 8.

6. Referring to "Set-in Seams" on page 15, join the star-point units to the squares.

a. Sew a star-point unit to the right-hand side of the square. Begin stitching at the inside corner and stop stitching ¼" from the outer edge. Backstitch carefully.

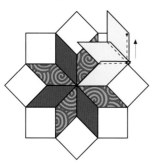

b. Sew the remaining side of the star-point unit to the adjacent square in the same manner.

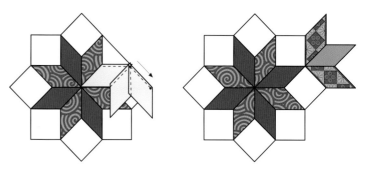

c. Attach the next star-point unit in the same way, then sew the two star-point units together. Stitch from the inside corner to the outer edge. Continue around the star until all 8 star-point units have been added and joined.

Join unit here.

7. Insert 8 Piece C ecru background triangles where indicated by the arrows in the diagram.

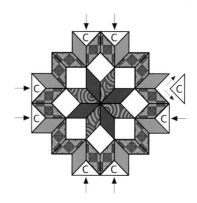

8. Attach 4 ecru background squares (Piece A) where indicated by the arrows. Follow the directions for adding squares in step 4

9. Attach 4 ecru background rectangles (Piece D) in the same manner you attached the squares, to complete the block.

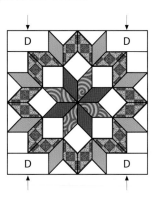

ROSE OF SHARON BORDER AND QUILT TOP ASSEMBLY

Bride
I am a rose of Sharon,
a lily growing in the valley.

Bridegroom
A lily among thorns
Is my dearest among the maidens.

Bride
Like an apple tree among the trees of the forest,
so is my beloved among young men.

The Song of Songs 2:1–3

Cutting

Cut and prepare the border appliqués, using the patterns provided on page 72 and the appliqué method of your choice. The freezer-paper method shown on pages 13–14 was used for the quilts in this book.

Directions

1. Assemble 2 strips, each composed of 3 completed blocks of your choice and 4 large and 4 small green print setting triangles.

Make 2.

2. Add these strips to the sides of the Tree of Life medallion.

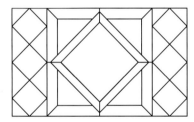

3. Assemble 2 strips, each composed of 5 completed blocks and 4 small and 8 large green setting triangles.

Make 2.

4. Add these strips to the top and bottom edges of the medallion.

5. Sew the strips for Border #4 together in pairs to make 4 long strips. Press the seams open.

6. If you cut each strip for Borders #3 and #5 in one long piece, mark the centers. If you cut them in 2 pieces, piece them together in sets of 2, being careful to match the design motif at each center seam. Trim the seam to ¼" and press open.

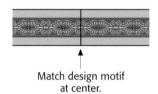

Match design motif
at center.

7. Attach each set of borders separately to the quilt top, mitering the corners as shown on pages 17–19. Carefully match centers and make sure all 4 corners on each striped border are identical.

Match design motif here.

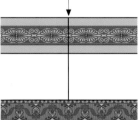

8. Position 3 Rose of Sharon appliqués along each side of the quilt as shown, with the flowers directly across from the outer corner of each block. Position an extra flower between each appliqué unit and at each corner of the quilt. Sew appliqués in place.

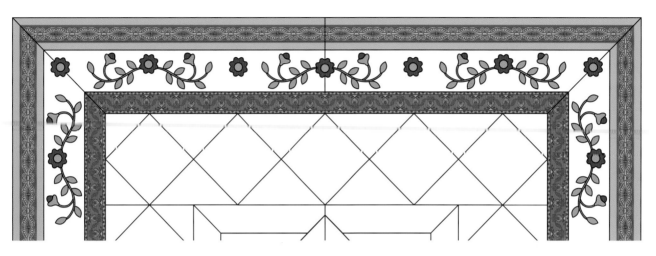

FINISHING THE QUILT

1. Press the completed quilt top carefully. Trim off any long threads.

2. Trace the quilting patterns from pages 73–78 onto the central medallion corner pieces and the setting pieces. Refer to the Quilting Pattern Placement Diagram on page 79 and to the photo of my quilt on page 10. Or if you prefer, you may echo the shape of these set pieces by drawing lines 1" apart, referring to the photo of Patricia Dear's quilt on page 5. Use a light table or a window and trace lightly with a quilter's pencil or chalk pencil. You may outline quilt the blocks and borders as desired. Mark quilting lines 1½" apart horizontally across the width of the appliqué border.

3. Layer the marked quilt top with batting and backing; baste.

4. Quilt.

5. Bind the edges of the quilt, referring to "General Directions" on page 12.

6. Sign your quilt or make a personalized label to attach to the back of the quilt at the lower right-hand corner. I also wrote the name of each pattern on the appropriate block so that anyone looking at the quilt would know what biblical reference each block represented. If you wish to do this, use a permanent marking pen.

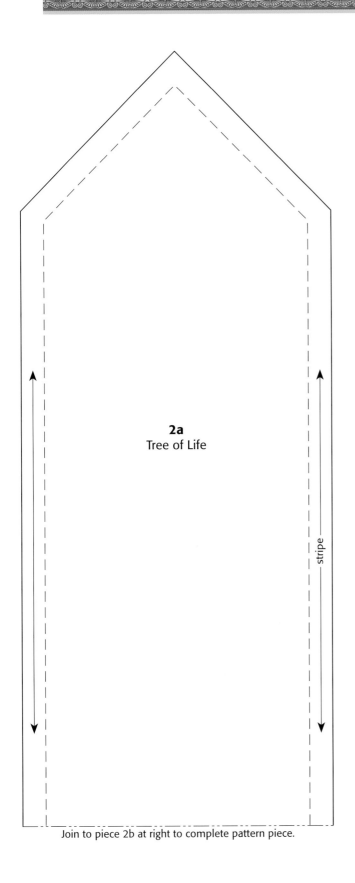

2a
Tree of Life

stripe

Join to piece 2b at right to complete pattern piece.

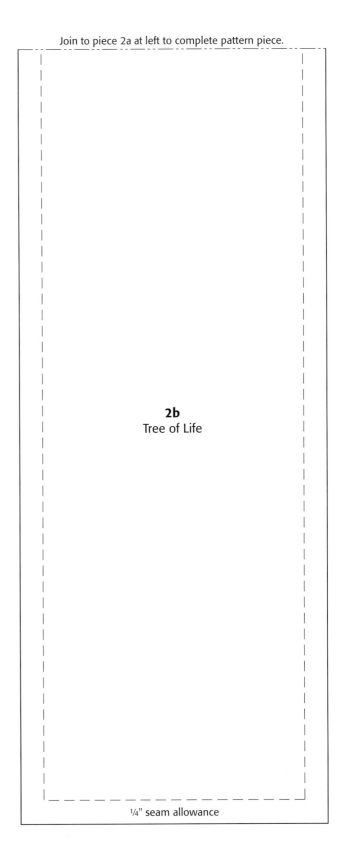

Join to piece 2a at left to complete pattern piece.

2b
Tree of Life

¼" seam allowance

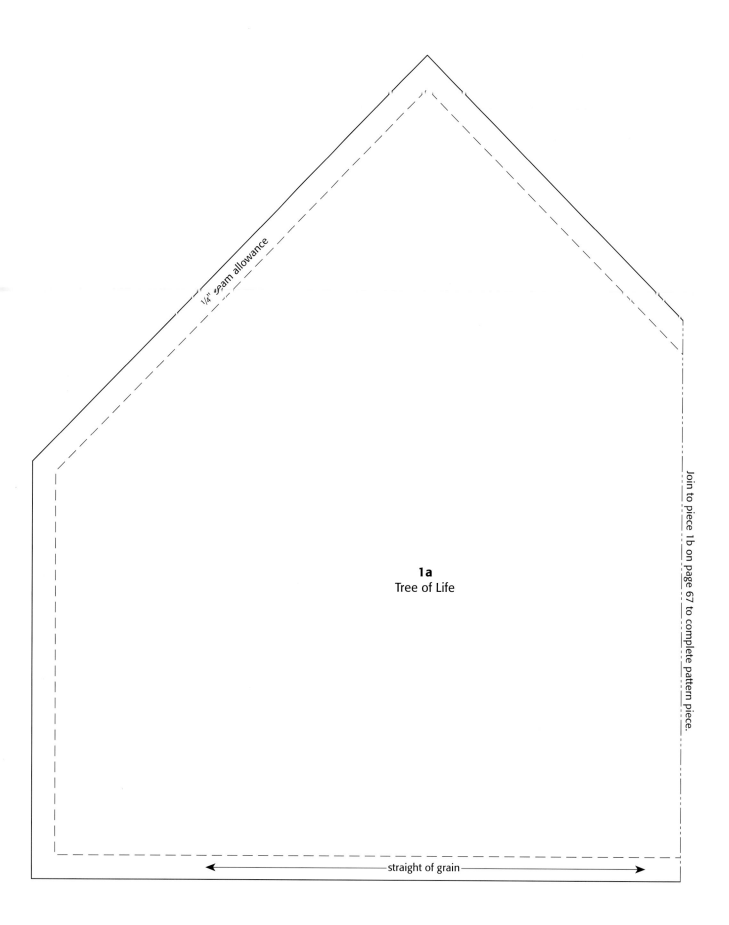

1a
Tree of Life

¼" seam allowance

Join to piece 1b on page 67 to complete pattern piece.

straight of grain

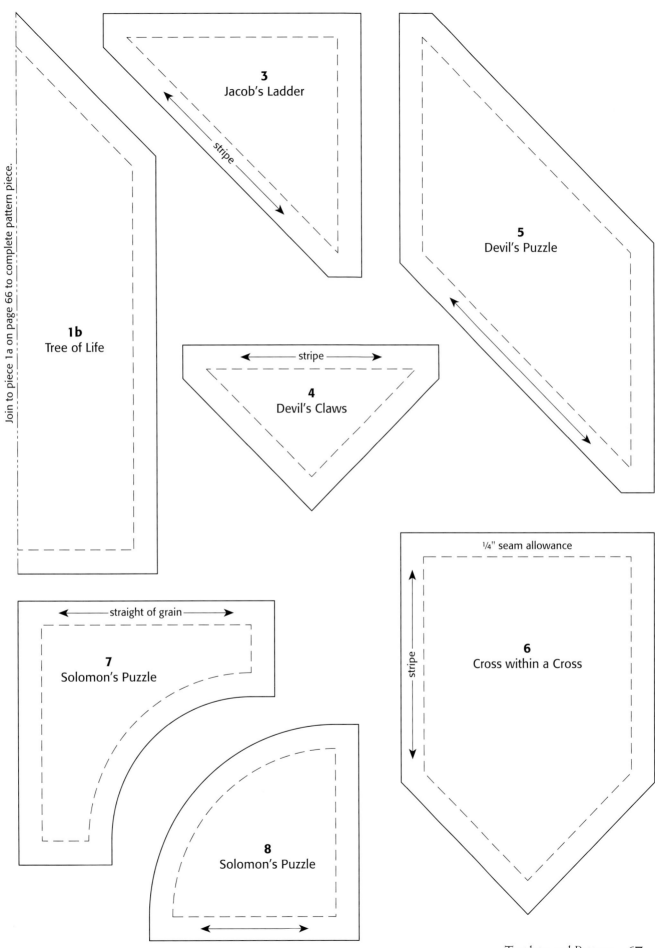

Join to piece 1a on page 66 to complete pattern piece.

1b
Tree of Life

3
Jacob's Ladder

stripe

5
Devil's Puzzle

stripe

4
Devil's Claws

7
Solomon's Puzzle

straight of grain

8
Solomon's Puzzle

6
Cross within a Cross

¼" seam allowance

stripe

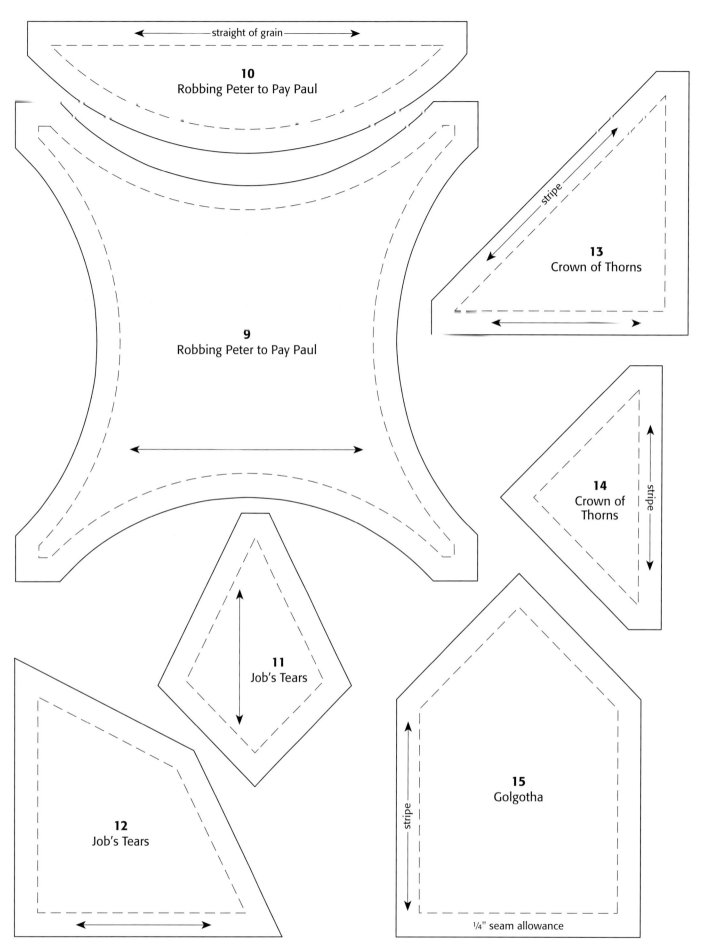

straight of grain

10
Robbing Peter to Pay Paul

9
Robbing Peter to Pay Paul

stripe

13
Crown of Thorns

stripe

14
Crown of Thorns

11
Job's Tears

12
Job's Tears

stripe

15
Golgotha

¼" seam allowance

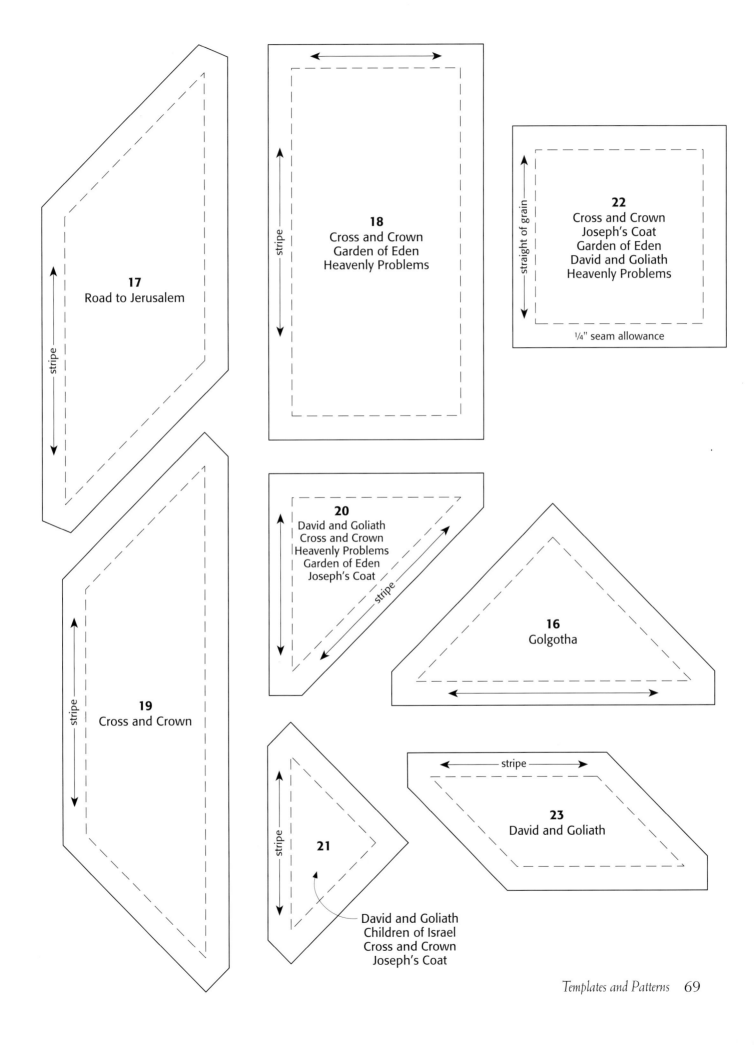

17
Road to Jerusalem

stripe

18
Cross and Crown
Garden of Eden
Heavenly Problems

stripe

22
Cross and Crown
Joseph's Coat
Garden of Eden
David and Goliath
Heavenly Problems

straight of grain

¼" seam allowance

19
Cross and Crown

stripe

20
David and Goliath
Cross and Crown
Heavenly Problems
Garden of Eden
Joseph's Coat

stripe

16
Golgotha

21

stripe

David and Goliath
Children of Israel
Cross and Crown
Joseph's Coat

stripe

23
David and Goliath

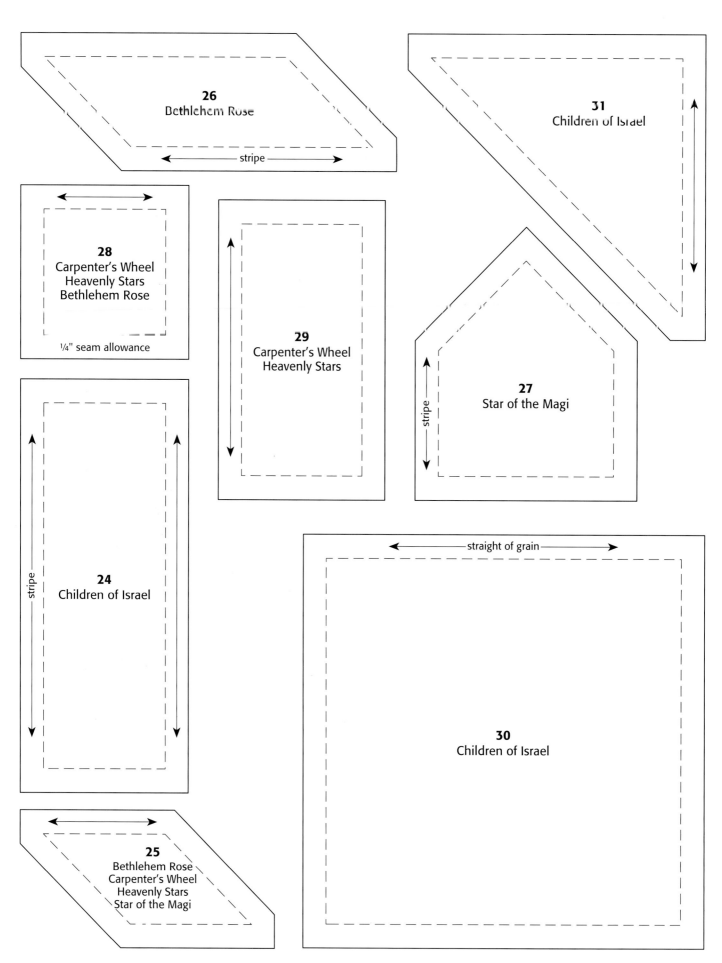

26
Bethlehem Rose

← stripe →

31
Children of Israel

28
Carpenter's Wheel
Heavenly Stars
Bethlehem Rose

¼" seam allowance

29
Carpenter's Wheel
Heavenly Stars

stripe

27
Star of the Magi

stripe

24
Children of Israel

straight of grain

30
Children of Israel

25
Bethlehem Rose
Carpenter's Wheel
Heavenly Stars
Star of the Magi

Foundation Pattern
Hosanna

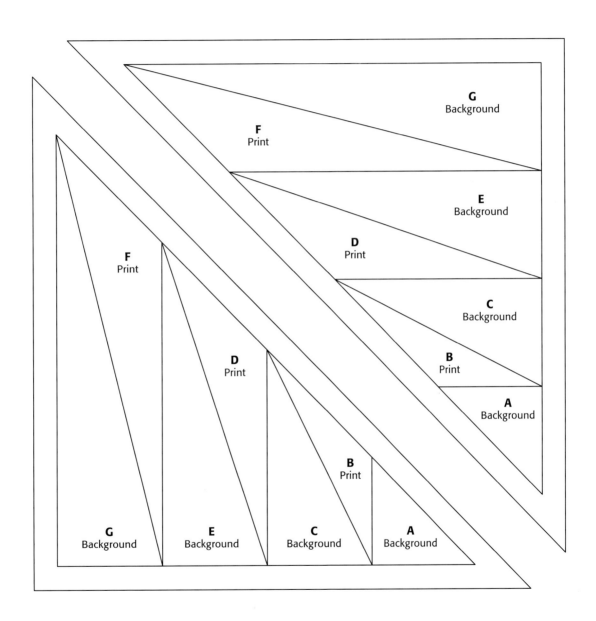

Rose of Sharon
Appliqué Pattern

Cut 144.

Cut 24.

Cut 24.

Cut 24.

Cut 24.

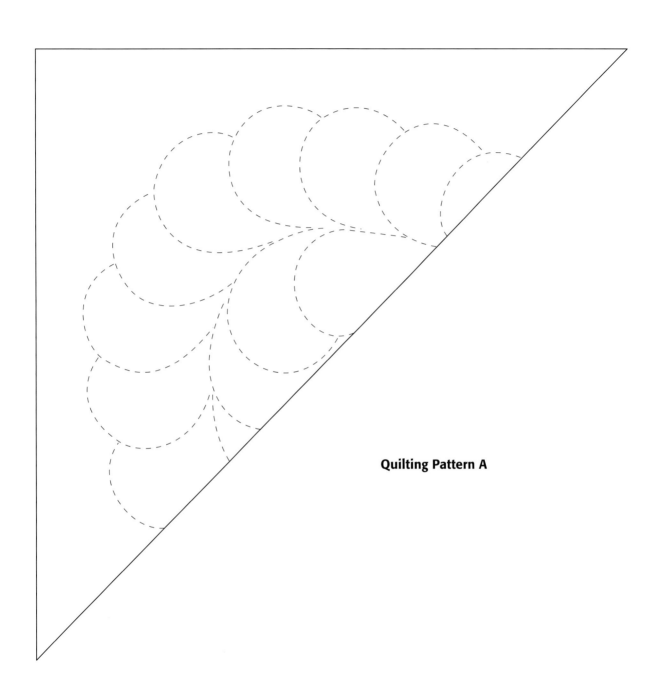

Quilting Pattern A

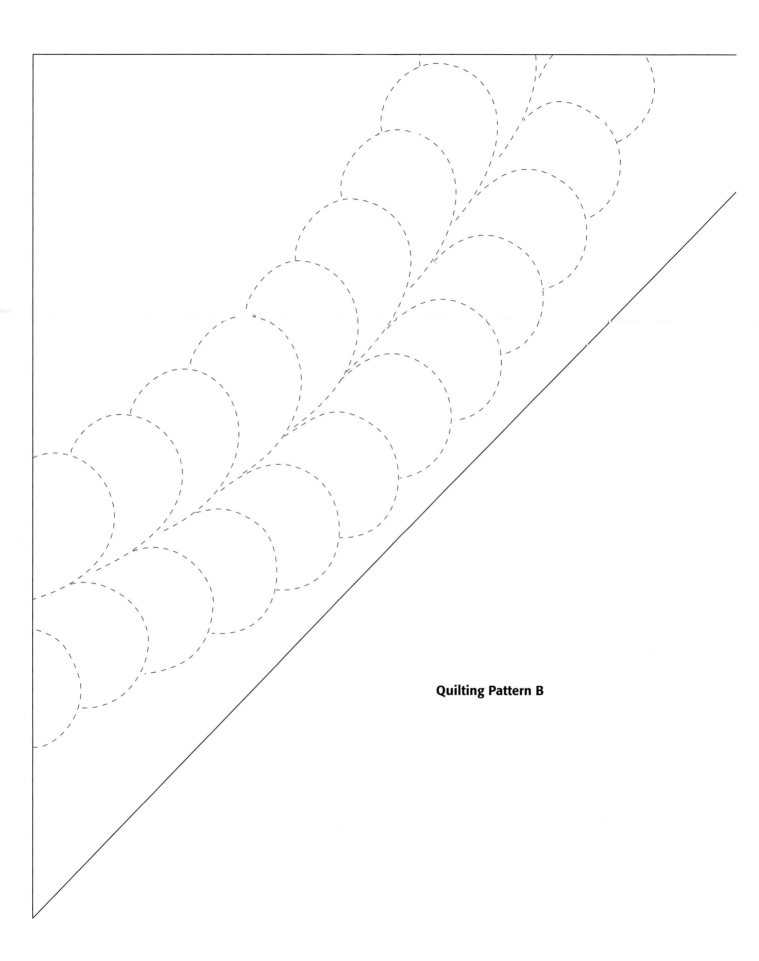

Quilting Pattern B

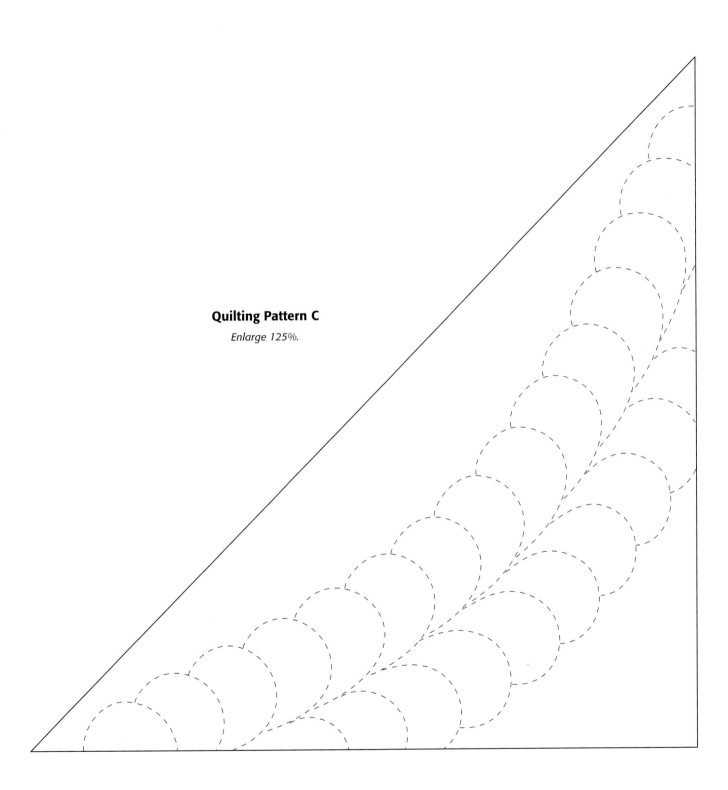

Quilting Pattern C

Enlarge 125%.

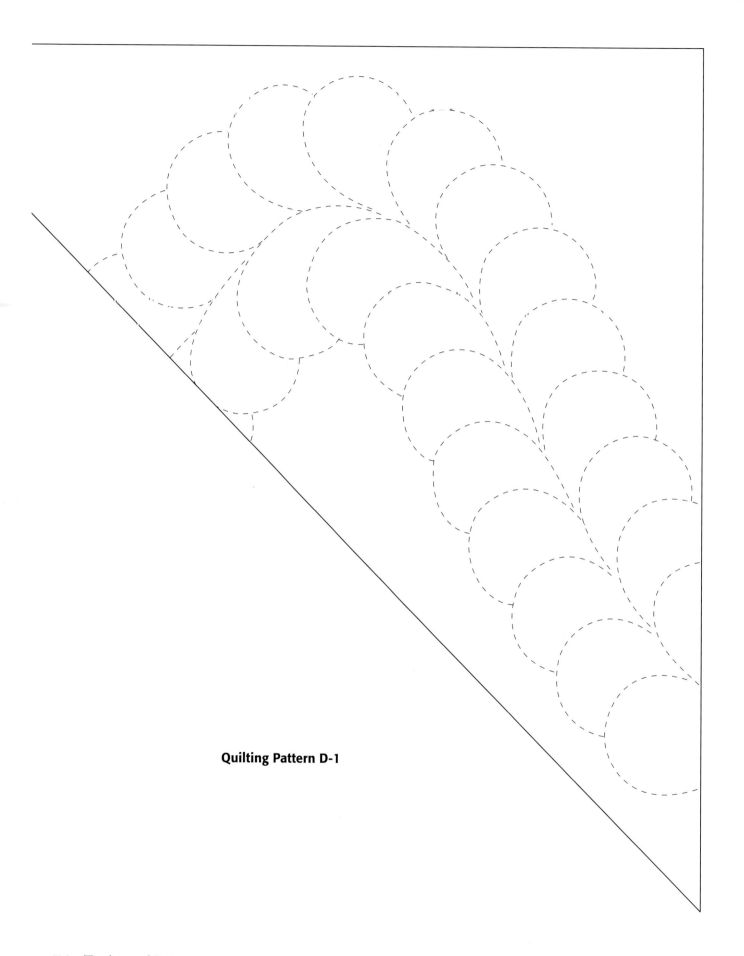

Quilting Pattern D-1

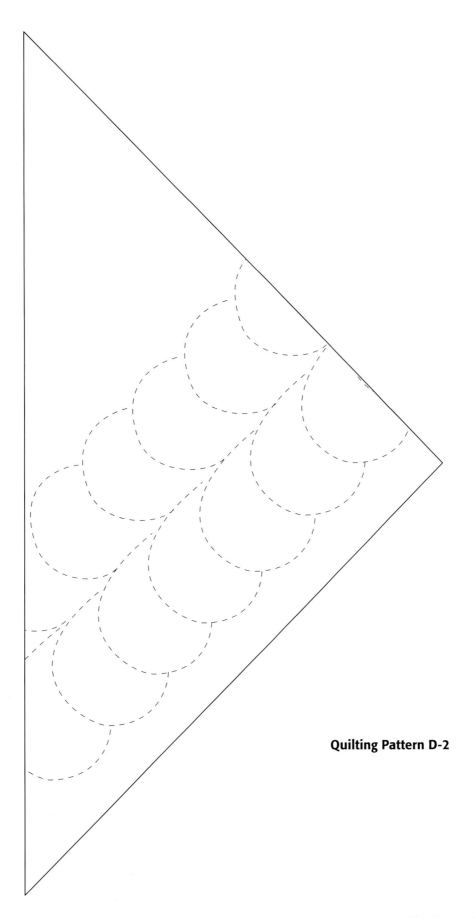

Quilting Pattern D-2

Quilting Pattern E

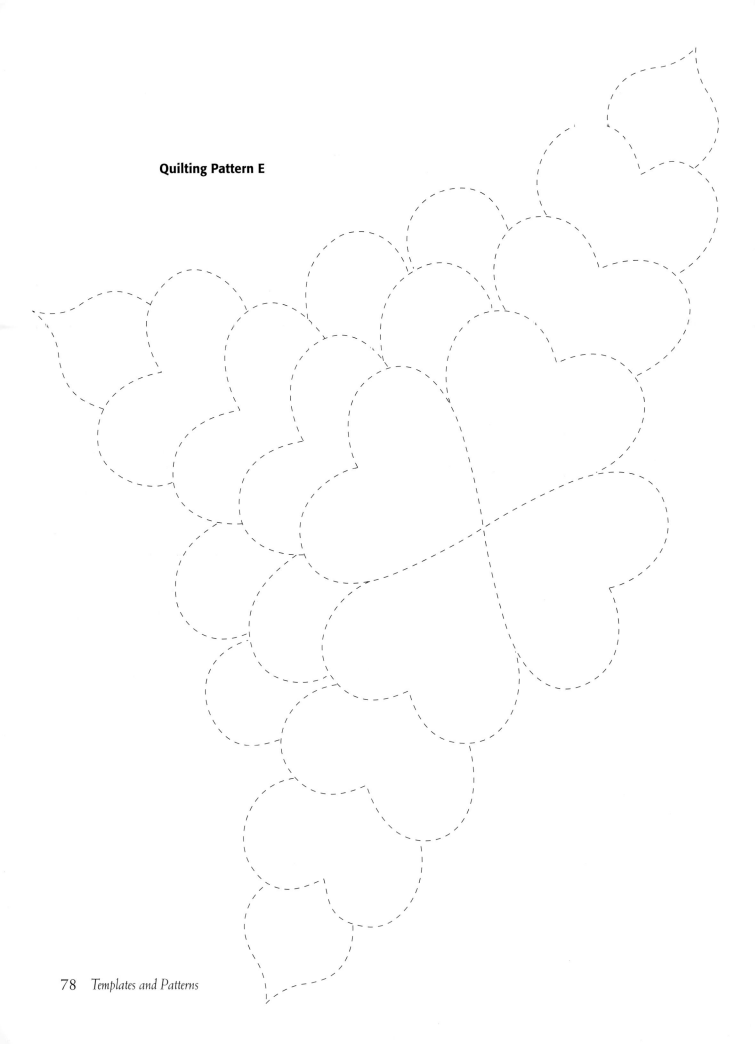

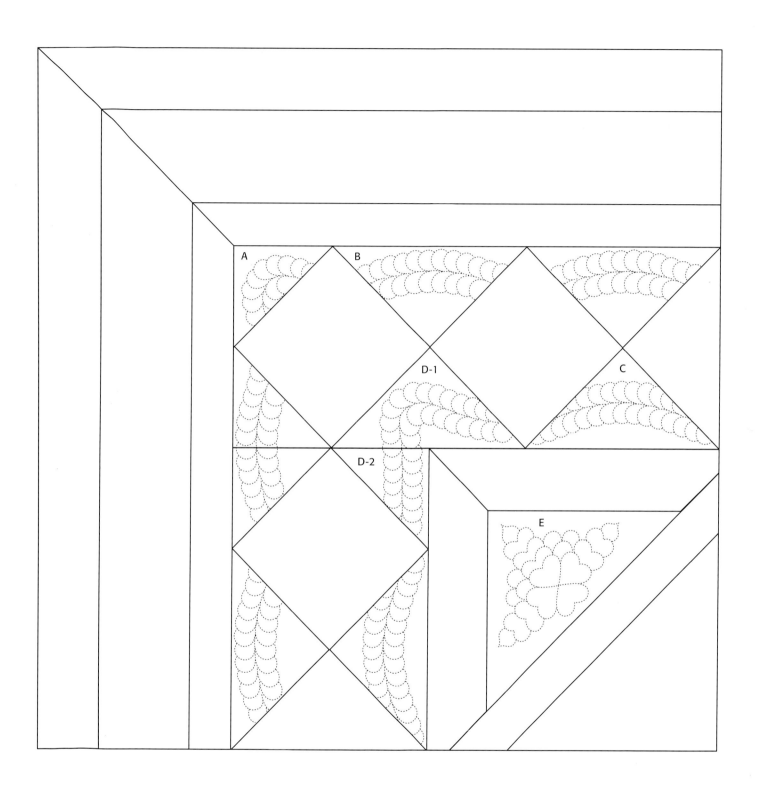

Quilting Pattern Placement Diagram

BIBLIOGRAPHY

Doak, Carol. *Show Me How to Paper Piece*. Bothell, Wash.: That Patchwork Place, 1997.

Makhan, Rosemary. *Floral Abundance*. Bothell, Wash.: Martingale & Company, 2000.

McCloskey, Marsha. *On to Square Two*. Bothell, Wash.: That Patchwork Place, 1992.

Thomas, Donna Lynn. *Shortcuts*. Bothell, Wash.: That Patchwork Place, 1991.

ABOUT THE AUTHOR

Rosemary Makhan grew up in Nova Scotia, Canada, where she learned the basics of quiltmaking from her mother. Her love of sewing and fabric led her to major in home economics at Nova Scotia Teachers College and at Acadia University. She taught high school family studies for several years.

Her interest in quiltmaking was rekindled when she made a baby quilt for her daughter, Candice, who likes to tell her friends that, if it weren't for her, her mother probably wouldn't have begun her quiltmaking career.

Rosemary taught adult education classes, becoming the founding president of the Halton Quilters Guild in 1977. She continues to teach many quiltmaking classes and workshops and enjoys the special fellowship and inspiration that come from working with quilters.

A traditional quiltmaker, Rosemary loves appliqué and makes many pieced quilts as well. She especially loves sampler quilts that are based on a theme, such as her Biblical Blocks, Samplings from the Sea, and Make Mine Country quilts. Often, the quilts she makes are her own design. If they are not, she changes or adds something to make them distinctive. She has created many patterns, including the popular Woodland Creature Collector Series, printed under her pattern label, "Quilts by Rosemary."

Each fall, Rosemary helps conduct a "Quilting in the Country" retreat for quilters in the picturesque Ontario countryside. She now lives in Burlington, Ontario, Canada, with her husband, Chris. They have two children, Candice and Kenneth.